Glory!
Hallelujah!

THE INNOVATIVE EVANGELISM OF EARLY CANADIAN SALVATIONISTS

I0132811

R.G. Moyles

Published by The Salvation Army, Canada and Bermuda Territory
2 Overlea Blvd., Toronto, Ontario M4H 1P4
Phone: 416.425.2111 Fax: 416.422.6120
www.salvationarmy.ca

Cover Design: Brandon Laird
Layout and Design: Brandon Laird

Printed in Canada
ISBN: 978-0-88857-504-3

The assistance of these contributors in preparing this book is greatly appreciated:
Members of the Territorial Literature Council, staff of the Editorial Department (Editor-in-Chief and Literary Secretary: Geoff Moulton)

TABLE OF CONTENTS

ACKNOWLEDGMENTS

MANY PEOPLE DESERVE MY THANKS FOR THEIR encouragement and help in bringing this publication to its successful completion. First, the staff of the George Scott Railton Heritage Centre for their untiring commitment to placing the Canadian *War Cry* online; it is a most valuable research tool and their initiative is to be highly commended. Second, Lt-Colonel Max Ryan diligently edited the manuscript and made many useful suggestions; his friendship and expertise are much appreciated. Thirdly, my wife, Ada, has read the whole several times and her discernment (as well as her love) can never be overestimated. Finally, I want to thank those in the Army's Editorial Department who have prepared it for publication. I hope they all said, "Glory! Hallelujah!"

INTRODUCTION

T HE SALVATION ARMY WAS, WITHOUT ARGUMENT, the most aggressive religious agency in the world of its time. "Every man, woman or child accepted as a recruit," wrote the Rev. Randall Davidson, "is supposed to become a centre of evangelizing work. One who has entered the hall out of sheer curiosity, or perhaps to scoff, is brought, before long, to kneel with bowed head at the 'penitent form.' Half an hour later he is bearing public testimony to the fact of his conversion, and that night or the next day sees him with a great 'S' upon his collar selling *The War Cry* in the streets and public houses, among the companions of his former life."

Davidson may have been exaggerating, but was essentially correct. William Booth, the Army's Founder, wanted every convert to become an active evangelist—"red-hot men and women who will stop at nothing" to seek the salvation of others. They were required to "go to the people with the gospel message," and do so in a manner that would, first, make them visible enough so that people would take notice, and, second, that would leave no doubt that the "salvation of souls" was their one and only object.

To that end, early Canadian Salvationists devised and engaged in many innovative means by which Booth's evangelistic mandate might be fulfilled. The open-air meeting was perhaps the most obvious, but beyond that Salvationists spread the gospel message in various ways: musical specials with such groups as the Kaleidoscopic Band or Welsh Minstrels; hallelujah weddings and summer camp meetings at which, sometimes, the whole community would be present. Under Evangeline Booth's command, one might be part of a travelling bicycle brigade, holding tent meetings in the summer in many towns throughout Ontario. And, in the larger community, a mountaineer brigade—Salvationists on horseback—would try to reach the lonely men and women of interior British Columbia; while along the coasts of the Great Lakes and Newfoundland and Labrador, Salvation Navies took the gospel to remote communities and outports. And, finally, when they were called to military service in the First World War—in the trenches of Ypres or Flanders—Canadian Salvationists conducted impromptu religious services, continuing their evangelism under the most dangerous conditions.

In the pages which follow, we will meet some of those Salvationists and vicariously experience their modes of evangelism. We shall witness some of the innovative ways by which they practised their religion and how they ministered. It is a story both exciting and inspiring. As those early Salvationists would say, "Glory! Hallelujah!"

ONE

"Novelty" Was Their Name

How Early Salvationists Attracted Their Converts

WHEN CANADA'S EARLIEST SALVATIONISTS—PEOPLE like Lieutenant Courts, Jack Addie, Joe Ludgate, Mr. and Mrs. William Freer and "Happy" Walter Bailey—began evangelizing the cities of Toronto and London, Ont., in May 1882, they did so in true Salvation Army style. They preached and testified in the open air, on street corners and in city parks. The open air was their spiritual battleground; or, to put it more felicitously, as William Booth did, the open air was the Army's cathedral. That was the manner in which he had started the Army, in the open air of the East End of London, England. "He stood up," wrote his biographer, Harold Begbie, "before the vilest people imaginable and proclaimed the gospel of love. He confronted the most abominable people in London, and denounced sin with the unqualified energy of an inspired prophet. He was fearless."

And he expected his officers and soldiers to be fearless, too. But it was not enough to be bold and brash—though that was the first requirement—it was as necessary to be innovative and inventive. So, as soon as The Salvation Army had established itself with a firm footing in Canada, its officers began to practise Booth's injunction with both daring and pleasure. That is, in addition to the ear-catching sounds of a big bass drum, or tambourines, or loud singing, or, later, brass bands (which were, of course, the main features of an open-air meeting), they often included some eye-catching features as well. Large placards, for example, proclaiming the Sunday's meetings in such extravagant language as "A Fight Against Old Nick" or "A Plunging in the Fountain" or "A Great Charge Against the Devil" were always effective. In addition, most effective were what Bramwell Booth called "sudden diversions"—imaginative play-acting to pique the interest of an indifferent crowd.

Imagine, for example, an Army open-air ring in which one soldier holds a large billboard announcing a "trial of the drum." While the meeting is in progress, a burly policeman enters the ring and immediately arrests, and then confiscates, the big bass drum. When the crowd follows him to the barracks, they witness a trial during which the policeman accuses the drum of various misdemeanors (such as being a public nuisance) while several witnesses support its benefits, saying they had been brought to the Army and conversion by its appeal. Not unexpectedly, the verdict comes down in favour of the drum, and the meeting is (and a later *War Cry* report says so) not only crowded but both stimulating and soul-winning.

When the Salvationists of St. Thomas, Ont., made it known through their open-air advertisements that they were going to auction off 13 children, the news soon got round and the barracks was filled for the event. While most realized that it was a sensational means of attracting a large attendance, there were some who seemed to believe that the 13 children were actually going to be sold to the highest bidders, as per advertisements. Even the astute chief of police was there, "to satisfy himself that nothing illegal was about to be perpetrated, ready to arrest the first person who purchased a good, all-wool, yard-wide $1.25 *youngster* at 99 cents." The building was, stated *The War Cry*, filled to its utmost capacity. And what the eager crowd witnessed was a mock auction in which bidders dressed to represent self-interest, sport, pleasure, wealth, education, nominal Christianity, fashion and, of course, true religion, each argued the advantages the children would enjoy should the auctioneer accept their bids. Naturally, he accepted none because, as he explained, wealth is deceptive, education is insufficient and nominal Christianity is a total failure. Only true religion provided for the highest welfare of the children, "both in this life and in the life to come," and so the 13 children became the property of true religion. "The whole proceedings were," concluded the *War Cry* report, "unique and original, and were enlivened by a well-performed children's drill."

In Saint John, N.B., the enterprising officer, Adjutant Sims, thought up this novel method of drawing a crowd. When he decided he would talk on "The Haunts and Jungles of Modern Babylon," from a tramp's point of view, he knew the best way to attract a crowd was to make the open-air meeting a mystifying and persuasive experience. In the middle of that meeting, "along came a ragged-looking tramp hooting and shouting, evidently trying to break up the gathering. The crowd which was fast gathering to see the trouble, suddenly observed a burly policeman rush into the circle of worshippers, seize the tramp and drag him down the street towards the barracks with a crowd at his heels. The peeler hurried the man into the hall and disappeared with him behind the private door, the crowd following into the hall. In a very few moments out stepped Adjutant Sims in the same tramp uniform, ready to address his expectant audience."

To modern readers, such antics might seem rather amusing—and no doubt more staid Christians of the time thought so, too—but evidence suggests they were quite effective in attracting attention. For, though conversions did sometimes take place at the open-air meeting itself, their main purpose was to entice people into the barracks to experience a red-hot revival meeting, the like of which they probably never experienced before.

GREAT SALVATION DUETT

THE

WELSH MINSTREL

AND

PROFESSOR WIGGINS

WONDERFUL COMBINATION

OF

MUSIC AND SALVATION

Great transformation of the Wicked
Welshman to the Singing Soldier and the
Drunken Professor to the Musical Possessor.

Hurricanes of Melody and Earthquakes of
Power

If the open-air strategies did not accomplish that aim, it was likely that the Saturday evening musical special would. Going head-to-head against such popular pastimes as the music hall and saloon, early Salvationists instituted the musical special both as an evangelistic outreach in its own right and as a sure means of drawing people to the next day's salvation meetings. Staged by a number of circulating variety groups at the local Orange Hall or opera house, they were so popular, the newspapers said, that nearly the whole town would spend an hour or two listening to religious music. And just as their handbills announced, the Hallelujah Quintette, Kaleidoscopic Band, Combination Salvation Company, All-Female Band (quite a novelty in that day) or even the Welsh Minstrels never failed to entertain, even as they presented the gospel by musical performance.

Two of the most versatile performers among the Army's many talented musicians were Staff-Captains George Wiggins and Richard Griffiths. The former was a graduate of London's Royal Academy of Music, excelled at the organ and, after a military career, taught music for a living. Drink had been his downfall, until he met The Salvation Army in Whitby, Ont., and experienced salvation and an entirely new

vocation. Similarly rescued from a life of drunkenness, Richard Griffiths, a Welshman and excellent violinist, also became one of the Army's musicians. The two sometimes performed alone, as a duet or as the leading musicians in groups loosely called the Welsh Minstrels or the Great Musical Company. At Saturday night festivals, from St. John's, N.L., to Vancouver, they gave vast audiences a taste of what they could expect at the Sunday salvation meetings. Here is how a reporter for the Peterborough *Examiner* (1887) described one of their Saturday evening's entertainments:

Talk of minstrel shows! They don't hold a candle to the Welsh

Minstrels. Saturday night the cheery tooting of several brass horns and the vigorous blowing of the "big bass drum" awakened the echoes of George Street, Peterborough, and attracted a large crowd. Sailing down the street came a long procession, headed by five men in flaming red jackets, with voluminous sashes of red, orange and blue, who were playing quick inspiriting tunes, such as *Good-bye, My Love, Good-bye, The Girl I Left Behind Me, Marching Through Georgia*, etc.—of course, though, to words of praise and adoration of the Great Redeemer. After the parade the barracks was filled with people at 10¢ a head, and if they didn't get their money's worth then, they never will. The usually staid and unpretentious platform was ornamented by an organ, a bass viol, a violincello and violin, which was afterwards augmented by a cornet. This comprised the stock-in-trade of the Welsh Minstrels. Staff-Captain Griffiths led the orchestra with his violin, Captain Connet the cornet, Ashton the bass viol, Dyker (alias Buffalo Bill) the violincello and "Professor" Wiggins the organ. And such music as they evolved from these instruments, and the vigour, the precision and fervour thrown into their singing by the soldiers. It just knocked out any philharmonic society, orchestra or any other musical organization in this district. The solos by the minstrels included several Satanic symphonies transposed to songs of glorification and thanksgiving.... But the amusing feature was the antics of Griff, the Welshman, who seems to have been born with an uncontrollable taste for minstrelsy in his mouth. Grasping his violin with the tenacity of a man who clutches his cudgel and prepares to bounce a midnight burglar, Griff would saw pitilessly on his unoffending fiddle for a few moments; then with a quick movement as though about to attack somebody, he would duck his head like a small man naturally would when dodging one of John L. Sullivan's blows, and extend both arms in a grappling motion; then, as if hesitating to begin the encounter, he would pirouette and "sashay," waving his arms "viciously" like the fans of a windmill, apparently to encourage his solders to fight and never run away; suddenly he would right about, face the foe, and with one fell swoop, amidst the crash of the orchestra and the thunder of the drum, assisted by the shriller tones of a hundred or more voices, totally annihilate the imaginary enemy's forces with a grand finale and conclusive dash of destruction.... Their visit proved as attractive as did that of General Booth; they are fine fellows, and it is to be hoped they will soon come again, as they expect to do.

Musical specials continued to enliven Army corps throughout Canada for many years. For a long while, Staff-Captain Griffiths remained the inspirational leader of many. In 1891, for example, he had organized the Musical Musketeers which included not only his wife, daughter and son, but, what was then a real novelty, a "coloured" singer and guitar player, Lieutenant Lee. She proved such an attraction that Commissioner Adams added her to his evangelistic retinue as he toured Canada in 1891. While he was doing so, the Kaleidoscope Brigade was touring Ontario, their tall hats becoming their trademark, and the source of much amusement and the question, "Where did you get that hat?" And while it was the hats which made them intentionally conspicuous, attracting the attention of those who otherwise might not have noticed them, it was their music—their brass band combination and their banjo playing and lively solos—which made their free-and-easy meeting a rouser and sent people away with fine memories of an evening at the local Orange Hall or the Salvation Army barracks.

As popular as the musical specials—and as effective both as entertainment and evangelism (so the newspapers said)—were the Army's hallelujah weddings. "To go to the Montreal Carnival," ran an advertisement, "will cost you a pile of money, and you will likely be disappointed. But if you want a good time, go to a hallelujah wedding." And, though today it may be surprising to read of Salvation Army weddings which drew thousands of people to witness them at 10 or 15 cents a head, that was indeed the case. So popular were they that local newspapers loved to describe them, as they did that of Captain "Happy" Bill Cooper, of Hamilton, Ont., and Captain Eliza Crosby, of Collingwood, Ont., in August 1884:

Reader, didst ever see a hallelujah wedding? Probably not. Well, in the first place, it may be said that the ceremony, in its essential points, differs very little from an ordinary marriage ceremony in the most staid and conservative church; but to the essentials are added peculiar accompaniments which make of the hallelujah wedding a ceremony which stands by itself as something wholly unique and inimitable.

It took place in the drill shed. The whole east end of the building was occupied by salvation soldiers and hallelujah lasses, sitting tier above tier, and packed close together, like spectators in a circus tent. Many of the soldiers and lasses had bannerets of blue, red and yellow, which they moved on the slightest provocation; a good many had tambourines which they pounded and jingled when noise was needed, and the remainder had handkerchiefs, which they kept in hand ready to move at a given signal. There were 400 or 500 Salvationists crowded together on those raised seats. There must have been 1,000 people in the building besides the Salvationists—and they paid 15 cents a piece to get in, too.

The bride was Captain Eliza Crosby, of Collingwood, and the bridegroom Captain Happy Bill Cooper, the irrepressible commanding officer of the Hamilton corps. Before the arrival of Major Moore (the American commander) and his staff, the Army amused itself by singing salvation hymns set to popular tunes and making merry remarks to each other. Presently a great shout arose from the soldiers, and all the occupants of the raised seats rose to their feet, and waved their tambourines, handkerchiefs, bonnets and banners, cheering vociferously. This demonstration meant that Major Moore and his staff had arrived. The enthusiasm had hardly subsided when a big man with a husky voice shouted: "Fire a volley for Major Moore!" and before he had got the words out there burst forth a storm of "hallelujahs!" and the banners, etc., were wildly waved again.

The real service was begun by a prayer from Rev. Mr. Thompson, the "saved parson," who, after 18 years in the Methodist ministry, saw the error of his ways, repented of his sins, and joined the Army. He offered up a rather curious invocation. "Oh, Lord," he said, "we know that you are not averse to weddings, for did you not go as a guest to the wedding at Cana in Galilee? Now we invite you here; we know you will come, and you will be welcome."

After the prayer two or three rousing hymns were sung. Major Moore then announced that the ceremony was going to take place, and immediately there was bustle and excitement among the spectators and a crush toward the platform. Soon the bride and bridegroom emerged from the crowd of officers and stood opposite each other, surrounded by their friends. Happy Bill's demeanour did not belie his name. His pale, livid face was wreathed with smiles. He stood in an easy, careless attitude, and all through the ceremony made funny remarks to those standing near, and occasionally would extend his arms to the soldiers with a request that they should "fire a volley," a request that always received a prompt response. The bride was not nearly as self-possessed as her chosen lord and master. She stood with drooping eyelids and head bent, but her face wore a quiet look of contentment. She is a nice-looking person with a trim figure and a demure pretty face.

Rev. Mr. Thompson now came forward and took Major Moore's position and read the regular marriage service of the Church of England. When he made his first response Happy Bill could not contain his enthusiasm, but as soon as he uttered in a sonorous voice the all-important "I do," he waved his arms towards the crowded seats and shouted, "Fire a volley!" Immediately the big building rang with "hallelujahs!" "amens!", the shrill voices of the women rising high over the men's bass roars. The Salvationists' cheer is something worth hearing. Talk about the "hearty British cheer," or "the wild American 'rah?"

When the time came to place the ring on the bride's finger, Happy Bill dived into his pocket for the loop of gold. He fumbled for a few seconds, and his face took on a look of anxiety; but presently he produced the ring. "The signet's all ready!" shouted Major Moore. A roar of laughter followed, and of course there was a scattering fire of "hallelujahs" from the brethren and sisters who could not see what was going on. After a while comparative silence was restored, and the ceremony was resumed.

"For better, for worse," said Bill, repeating the words after the saved parson.

"There's no worse about it!" shouted the major, and the uproar broke out afresh.

The bridegroom then grasped the hand of his bride and vigorously pushed the ring on her third finger, and as he held her hand lingeringly he repeated after the parson the words to the effect that he bestowed upon her all his "worldly goods." As he uttered the words he laughed outright at the ridiculousness of the idea. Major Coombs shouted ironically: "He gives her all his worldly goods! Why, he hain't got none!"

Another outburst of laughter and cheers followed this remark and the ceremony was finished before the hubbub subsided. Only the concluding words from the parson were heard: "Whom God hath joined together let no man put asunder." Then followed a perfect whirlwind of cheers, all the occupants of the raised seats rising to their feet. Waving their arms and straining their throats to the utmost. Even the spectators caught the infection, and to their own surprise found themselves shouting, too. After about five minutes Rev. Mr. Thompson read that portion of Scripture which sets forth the duties of wives to the husbands and of husbands to their wives. When this was concluded the brass band struck up a lively air which they played through several times without variations. Major Moore then stepped forward with a large Bible, which he placed in the hands of the bridegroom. He explained to the audience that Happy Bill had earned it, for it was the custom of the Army to present a Bible to the first officer married in a division, and Bill was the first who had been married in Hamilton.

That wedding ended, as did most, with testimonies from the bride and groom, followed by a great deal of singing, a solo or two, and, finally, by "hallelujah tea-and-cake." One reporter had this to say: "I came away feeling that however peculiar these people may be they bring everything, marriages included, to the point they have in view, viz: getting people made good. The newly married couple gave an address, each urging the audience to come and get saved. That's not bad is it for a wedding speech.... If ever I get married, and I have since this affair been seriously thinking the matter over, I shall most likely ask the Army to officiate, and if God and myself are satisfied, I think every one else should be the same. By the way, Mr. Editor, I rather like these hallelujah weddings and I might just mention that I did not see anything at all repulsive in the bonnets."

Getting people made good. That was what it was all about—even the weddings. When Adjutant Tom Southall and Captain Jennie Langtry were married in the roller rink in Saint John, N.B., as many as 4,000 people, so *The War Cry* said, attended the "hallelujah celebration."

"Through the fog and the mist," wrote a reporter for the Saint John *Telegraph*, "they rallied from every section of the city and packed the great auditorium to overflowing. Two thirds of them were ladies. They occupied the seats in the body of the hall. Five hundred men and a score of hoodlums line the sides, and a select assortment of small boys roosted on the roof and looked in at the windows.... Anyone who was there will tell you that he got his ten cents' worth."

Why? Because, though religious in intention, it was entertaining and uplifting. There were solos by "little Harry Morris, who has a very sweet voice" and by Adjutant Bolton, former minstrel, "who hasn't forgotten how to handle a tambourine," and who, on this occasion, said he meant to teach the people how to spell:

It's g-l-o-r-y to know
I'm s-a-v-e-d;
I'm h-a-p-p-y because
I'm f-r-double-e.
Once I was b-o-u-n-d
In the chains of s-i-n,
But v-i-c-t-o-r-y

Through Christ I'm sure to win.

Between the verses, the energetic captain danced a hallelujah jig, and called upon the audience to wave their handkerchiefs and join in the song, and "not be too respectable." It was, as the newspapers averred, a "grand festive occasion." And there was no doubt in the reporter's mind: if you wanted music in your soul and joy in your heart, there was no better place to get it than at a hallelujah wedding.

"We mean to show everybody that we are a happy, hallelujah people, giving glory to God through everything we do," stated one Salvation Army officer. And, though critics might liken its methods to vaudeville or the circus, The Salvation Army proved, by the immense popularity of those methods, that people saw the true purpose behind them and responded with eagerness to them.

When early Canadian Salvationists marched through city streets and stood at street corners to hold open-air meetings, or when they entertained thousands at a Saturday night musical special, or even when they got married, they had one purpose in mind—to make known the good news of the gospel. They hoped that the jubilance of their music and singing, the sheer joy they displayed and the novelty of their diversions would draw people to the barracks where their style of red-hot revivalism might convince them of their need of salvation and, as important, persuade them to become soldiers in the Army.

For of one thing Salvationists were quite certain: if the open-air meetings and the musical specials managed to draw people to the barracks, the Army's exuberant style of worship—so akin to early Methodism in its near-charismatic fervour and so different from Anglicanism in its spontaneity and freedom—would compel them to a permanent commitment to Christ. Why? Well, let's visit one such meeting to find out.

But first a reminder. There was no such thing as a typical Salvation Army meeting. There were, in the first place, several kinds: the morning holiness meeting, the free-and-easy afternoon meeting, the evening salvation meeting as well as special prayer meetings, all-night prayer meetings and anniversary meetings. Each of these might exhibit different characteristics. Moreover, the personality of the officer-in-charge would significantly determine the tone of the meeting. And, finally, the nature of the congregation affected the overall tone of the meetings; the Salvationists of Newfoundland, for example, being of a more charismatic inclination than those in Ontario. Having said that, we can identify enough similarities in all those meetings to suggest that the one we attend would have been very much like any other. Let's go and find out.

To us, church-going strangers that we are, the barracks seems rather bare and uninviting—no statuary, no stained-glass windows, no baptismal font—just a plain meeting house with some striking posters on the walls—"Jesus Saves!" and "Now is the Moment!" and "Where Will You Spend Eternity?" At the front there is a raised platform with seats, as yet empty (for all the soldiers are "on the march"), with two large pictures of General William Booth and his wife, Catherine. Nothing more.

As we enter, at the inside door stands a comely-looking man with a collection basket containing a few pennies. We take the hint and add slightly to its sum total which means, we think, that no other collection will be taken. Inside there is a seeming confusion: people are talking and laughing, and introducing their friends, and soon we are welcomed (over and over again, with enough greetings of "God bless you" to last us all the week). Some pretty Salvation lasses are circulating, selling the *Soldiers' Song Book* at just 10¢ ("You'll need it for the singing!") and *The War Cry* for another 3¢, both of which we buy. *The War Cry*, by the way, appears to be one of the main sources of the Army's revenue—some 25,000 copies being sold each week in Ontario alone.

Within 30 minutes the blood-washed warriors (as they style themselves) come trooping into the barracks, singing and shouting such slogans as "Hallelujah!" and "Bound for glory!" Some of them are carrying musical instruments, and they seat themselves in a separate group, after having dropped to their knees for a brief prayer. The other soldiers, all having knelt to pray, as well, take up the remaining space on the platform. While waiting for their leader, a female captain, to take her place, they strike up a chorus, singing, "Follow, follow, I will follow Jesus. Everywhere he leads me I will follow on." With every inch of space fully occupied, the whole congregation joins in. It seems many of them are thoroughly familiar with the lyrics, and we realize after they have sung it once through, are easily remembered.

When the captain, in her trim uniform of navy blue with red braid and plain black broad-brimmed bonnet with the words "The Salvation Army" on its red band, takes her place, the singing subsides and she takes command. She is a genteel-looking woman of perhaps 27 or 28 years of age, and begins as follows: "Well, my friends, I'm glad there'll be plenty of room in heaven; plenty of room, too, in the heart of Jesus for each and all of us. There'll be no crowding and jostling there. Now be as patient as you can, those of you who are standing, and we'll commence our service by singing song number 75 in the *Soldiers' Song Book*. Now let us sing this song with our whole strength as unto God."

And we do. With the brass band accompanying, tambourines rattling and many hands clapping, we sing a rousing song to that great martial air, *Marching Through Georgia*:

Shout aloud salvation, and we'll have another song;
Sing it with a spirit that will start the world along;
Sing it as our comrades sang it many a thousand strong,
As they were marching to glory.

March on, march on! we bring the jubilee;
Fight on, fight on! Salvation makes us free;
We'll shout our Saviour's praises over every land and sea
As we go marching to glory.

The stirring strains of that song thrill every nerve. The *paean* gathers strength and force as it proceeds; and soon the dense volume of sound pouring from the throats of almost a thousand men and women, singing with all their might, seems to shake the old barracks to its very foundation. The effect is simply tremendous.

Then a very curious thing. As they are singing the last verse, almost the last lines of the chorus, all the soldiers (and some who are not, we presume) drop to their knees. As soon as the song is finished, they start to sing softly and sweetly "Oh, Calvary, dark Calvary, speak to my heart from Calvary!" Then follow prayers from all over the building, of intense feeling and of great power. When this is followed by another song, *Rescue the Perishing*, all still in the kneeling position, the effect, though peculiar, is very thrilling indeed.

The prayers are earnest, often colloquial. One woman prays fervently: "O Lord, I thank you that I am able to be here at all to testify for Jesus. You know I have been sick nearly all week, and that I have had a very bad cold even today, and that if you had not helped me I could not have had strength enough to come out now. I have been grieving all week that I could not do more work for Jesus, but you know it was not my fault."

The prayers ended, the captain rises again, and in a quiet conversational tone—every word, however, being distinctly audible in every part of the hall—reads a short passage of Scripture on which she comments very eloquently. Her manner is perfectly natural and free from restraint, and she is evidently conscious, yet with all becoming modesty, of her ability to control and attract her audience. The simple, unaffected eloquence of this comparatively uneducated woman goes straight to the heart, and she holds her vast assemblage spellbound by the charm and magic of her earnestness and feeling. When the captain ceases, many an eye is dimmed and many a cheek is wet with the tear that wells unbidden from its secret source. Truly the scene is one not to be forgotten.

Then follows what they call "a glorious free-and-easy" or, as the captain termed it, a period of witness. It was the single feature of the meeting that we looked forward to, for we had read, somewhat earlier, an article by the noted Canadian poet, Agnes Maule Machar, in which she described the testimony period, with its interspersion of lively choruses, as the chief attraction of Salvation Army meetings. They lend, she said, a perpetual freshness and keep the halls filled, night after night. She continues: "After the singing has had its effect on both the audience and the 'soldiers,' the latter are desired by the 'captain' to 'fire away,' these testimonies being considered, in 'Army' phraseology, the 'red-hot shot,' while the music, etc., are the 'powder and cartridges.' There is no false shame among the Army converts. Every soldier casts aside that, along with other fear, when he or she takes a seat on the platform. There are usually two or three waiting their turn to speak. And they speak with a simplicity, directness and force which evidently comes from the heart, and consequently goes to the heart. Each testifies to his gladness in 'being saved,' to his daily experience of the life-giving and strength-giving power of the personal Christ received into the soul; and simple, often rude and ungrammatical as the language is, there is a power about it that strength of conviction and intensity of feeling always supply. That young men and women, but a short time before as giddy, as reckless or dissipated, as any of their companions, should have the courage and power to stand up before a crowded assemblage of their own class, and declare what a change the accepted love of God has wrought in their own hearts and lives, appears to most of the hearers little short of miraculous.... As each 'soldier' finishes his 'testimony,' it is usual for the 'captain' to strike in with an appropriate verse of a hymn in which all join, sometimes repeating a chorus over some eight or 10 times, just as the impulse directs, while one or two more stand waiting to speak until the hymn is finished. There is no routine, and, within certain limits, variations are constantly occurring, so that at least there is no fear of monotony."

No fear of monotony, indeed! And certainly no reluctance on the part of the soldiers. Often after each chorus, several were waiting to testify. One convert tells that 18 months ago he was a miserable drunkard—"primed with whiskey from Monday morning until Saturday night, and on Sunday little better. But The Salvation Army got hold of me, and I thank God for it. Go to my home and ask there if this salvation has done anything for them and for me. My wife and family will tell you something that will make you stare. In my workshop, where I used to curse and swear with my workmen—not men of my own age but youths, some of them mere lads—I can now speak a word of warning; I can tell them of the love of Jesus; I can set an example in the other direction. Yes, I am thankful the Army ever came to Toronto."

No one is allowed to occupy more than two or three minutes, and the majority are content with a less liberal allowance of time. Occasionally, however, someone will forget himself, but a warning word from the captain—"Now, that will do, we'll have to sing you down"—never fails to cut off the flow of eloquence in short order. In fact, one middle-aged woman, after a short exhortation, looked as if she would continue for some time, when the captain rose quickly, and with a sudden authoritative wave of the hand towards the speaker, struck up, "I'm saved I am, I know I am! I'm washed in Jesus' blood." Immediately everybody united to sing two or three stanzas. Then she turns to the back row of the seats—"Now another of you up there give us your experience and be brief. You, a week old, let's hear from you. We've heard from the yearlings, now for the weekling." And so they move along, speaking, singing, praying. At one point they even had a "wave offering," when all those who know their sins forgiven were asked to pull out their handkerchiefs and wave them to and fro to the lively music of a "waving chorus." Many in the audience, seeing the force of the idea, responded with equal enthusiasm, even waving the *War Cry* in their desire to bless Jesus' name. All this, until the "free-and-easy" has exhausted its time.

What strikes one most forcibly is that a Salvation Army meeting is a participatory affair. Undoubtedly clericalization will set in, but right now it seems that they firmly hold to the idea of the priesthood of all believers. I was told that William Booth did not approve of the notion that the officer would do all the fighting and feeding, while the congregation would do all the looking and swallowing. And that is why, I suppose, the soldiers not only fully participated by their clapping and vociferous "hallelujahs" and "amens!" but with their prayers, their testimonies and, during the testimony period, with their frequent introduction of choruses.

It was boisterous, but seemingly joyful, and certainly always heartfelt.

Before leaving this aspect of the meeting, I must say something about the singing and music. While some of the songs and choruses would have been familiar to anyone who had attended a religious camp meeting—being of the Sankey and Moody kind—many of them were entirely new, though the tunes to which they were set were familiar as being taken from old folk and music-hall songs. Thus, while they sang (over and over) "It's the old-time religion" and "Oh, what will you do, brother (sister, and so on), when he comes?" (With the refrain "Oh, the Army will be ready when he comes"); they sang

"I'm glad I'm a Salvation soldier/I promise to stand firm and true/To the flag with the star in the centre/The yellow, the red and the blue." This they sang with such gusto, over many times, while someone took the flag ("the yellow, the red and the blue") from its bracket and waved it about. It was very exciting to listen to. And then, later, they sang a beautiful chorus, *Bless His Name He Sets Me Free*, to that familiar music-hall tune, *Champagne Charlie*. It seemed at first, slightly sacrilegious, but, after it was sung a few times it was truly enjoyable, and if one concentrated on the "converted" words, one entirely forgot the music-hall associations. The Army, they said, has a lot of those songs, and that must certainly be what many people come to the meetings to hear. And, before I forget, if one likes brass-band music, its accompaniment to the songs was truly inspirational. For the choruses the band was silent, and the louder accompaniment of drums, tambourines and, in this case, a concertina augmented the singing.

After the meeting had lasted for an hour and a half or two hours, the leaders and the soldiers came down from the platform and knelt on the floor of the hall in a perfectly informal prayer meeting for the salvation of souls. This is what they call the after meeting. Many of those who had come out of curiosity, or for the pleasure of the main meeting, now left the barracks (though I noticed quite a few were sufficiently impressed by the whole to stay to the end: they were, to use an angling phrase, hooked). The captain and her lieutenants, and some of the soldiers as well, now went about, talking earnestly to the more interested few who remained, and persuading one and another to take the decisive steps of coming forward to kneel as a penitent confessing sin and asking for salvation, while, all the time, earnest prayers are being offered for their souls, in the most direct and simple phraseology.... These after meetings are the time when, in Army phraseology, prisoners are taken and converts, by taking the step of coming forward, confess their faith and their desire henceforth to serve Christ. To some natures such an external register of an inward resolve is a great help, and certainly in the case of almost all the Army's converts, they henceforth are "not ashamed to confess the faith of Christ crucified, and to fight under his banner against sin, the world, and the devil, and to continue Christ's faithful soldiers and servants unto their life's end."

I have, since that meeting, read in one of our religious magazines, *The Canadian Independent*, a personal account by a Salvationist of how they encourage (though that is the polite word, some say) people to seek salvation—to accept Jesus Christ as their Saviour and, by his help, lead a new life (and possibly become Salvationists):

Editor: One Sabbath afternoon, I was up among the praying circle at the front (and they don't look for anything to lean on, but just drop down on the floor anywhere). From there I got my eye on a man I thought I could influence, a little afraid to make the attempt, for fear I should lose what little influence I had over him. I bowed down my head again in prayer, that God would strengthen me and give me arguments, and incline *him* to listen. There was somebody earnestly praying aloud; and the man was evidently listening; for when I looked up again there were tears glistening in his eyes. I felt that my prayer was answered, and that this was the sign of it to me! I went straight and sat down beside him. "Well, Mr. P—you and I are getting old. We must soon be face to face with the question of eternity!"

"Yes, that is true, we shall."

"And how important to be ready! To have our sins washed away by Christ, and be ready to meet him, I am ready; I don't know whether you are."

"Not as ready as I would like to be!"

"Well now, I'll stick by you; I won't leave you. Come up to the front, and let us kneel down together, and pray for a blessing. Come!" And he just came up like a lamb; and we knelt down together at the penitent bench. I prayed; and soon *he* prayed and with a little instruction as to Christ's atonement, and willingness, and power, he then and there gave himself away; and said he "could trust his soul with *him* now!" And at the end of the meeting, the man's wife came up and joined him, radiant with happiness.

One learns how to speak to the impenitent. One good way of approaching them, is to ask kindly, "Are you serving God?" They are pretty sure to admit in somewhat direct terms (not seeing to what it will lead) that they are not. Then ask them, with great kindness and solemnity (never mind the grammar!): "Then who *are* you serving?" The application is irresistible; for if not serving God, they are serving the devil. Perhaps they never thought of it in that light before. And though perhaps no visible impression is made at the moment, a week or two after we hear them testify to the grace of God, and tell how someone talked to them, and showed them they were slaves to the devil's service.

Thus ends our visit to an early Salvation Army meeting. It has been, to say the least, edifying. The two hours passed very enjoyably: here was a freedom of expression, a sincerity and joy, all kept within the bounds of decency and order. I say that most emphatically because there are many people—whose opinions are often expressed in newspapers and religious magazines—who believe that all Salvation Army meetings are rowdy and irreverent affairs. They say that Army meetings are intended to excite the emotions; that Salvationists (especially the officers) use low language when they talk of bringing the glory down or of boiling over with Holy Ghost power. Low words, says Cardinal Manning (who has never been to an Army meeting), generate low thoughts: "Words without reverence destroy the veneration of the human mind. When man ceases to venerate, he ceases to worship." To attempt to feed people on extravagances, says another, is like keeping the body sustained by stimulants; it will result in premature death.

There may be some validity to those opinions. For I expect, from what I have read, that there are Army meetings—depending on the purpose and the inclination of the presiding officer—which border on the hysterical. But I think that must be the exception to the rule. In any event, I would characterize the meeting we attended as simply a joyous affair; noisy to be sure, with many uncultured features (for many, but not all, of the converts were lower-class people; just the people the Army say they hope to redeem); and somewhat weak in theology as well. But, the fervency of the prayers, the poignancy of the testimonies, the exuberance of the singing and the simple (yet eloquent) sermonette from the captain, all combined to create a spirit of devotion. And I end by saying this: The apparent familiarity, the free and easiness with which those Salvationists address the deity, appears to me to result from their extraordinary vivid realization of his continued presence. Ordinary worshippers only approach God occasionally, and when they do they feel it a solemn thing to enter his presence, and accordingly a thing to be done with due ceremony. The Salvationists, so it seems to me, in all their proceedings never for a moment lay aside their consciousness that they are in the immediate presence of the deity. They never enter his presence because they never quit it.

NOTE: The preceding descriptions are based on actual accounts of Salvation Army activities and meetings. See, for example, the following:

Agnes Maule Machar, "Red Cross Knights of The Salvation Army," *Andover Review*, 2 (1884): 193-210.

Anon, "The Salvation Army," *The Christian Guardian* (August 12, 1884).

Anon, "The Salvation Army," *The Independent* (August 1, 1886).

TWO

"Come and Hear a Woman Preach"

The Evangelistic Success of the Female Preacher

W ITH NO DISRESPECT TO THE MANY MALE OFFICERS of The Salvation Army who undertook the evangelization of Canada with both courage and dedication, it is generally acknowledged that William Booth's equal employment of female officers (comprising half of the total officer contingent) was a chief reason for the Army's remarkable success in its early decades. Booth generously acknowledged that fact when he stated at the beginning of the Army's progress that, though some said women would be the ruin of his Mission, he was convinced "that the prosperity of the work in every respect just appears most precisely at the very times when female preachers are being allowed the fullest opportunity." And, it is well known that he would often aver that "women were his best men."

That was proven time and again in Canada, as female officers, in twos and threes, "invaded" many of the small towns of Ontario, and then travelled east and west to "bombard" the hard-rock places where either men dominated or opposition had to be quelled. In 1887, for example, Mr. William Sproston Caine, a member of the British House of Commons, undertook a world tour, beginning with a trip across Canada to Vancouver. In September of that year he stopped at Calgary and besides hobnobbing with local ranchers and cowboys (and interviewing some Indians), he attended a Salvation Army meeting, the Army then having been in that prairie town but a single month. This is how he described his evening:

> The popular amusement [in Calgary] is The Salvation Army,
> conducted by a captain and three comely young women, who
> were treated everywhere with marked respect. They
> marched round the town in their usual fashion, passing
> through crowds of cowboys and similar young fellows,
> without encountering a jeer or a coarse word. When they
> entered their barracks all the men in the place swarmed in
> after them, to the tune of 500 or 600, took their seats quietly,
> joined heartily in the choruses of the hymns, which they
> seemed to know by heart, and evidently enjoyed themselves
> thoroughly. The Salvation Army young ladies were cordially
> welcomed by a clapping of hands. The meetings seemed to

have been successful, for there were arranged in a row on the platform, a dozen young fellows of the cowboy pattern, who had been converted at previous meetings, and who gave their experience in simple, and sometimes very touching sentences. One of them was received by the whole audience with several rounds of warm applause, and cries of "Bravo, Ted!" I was informed that Ted was the champion rowdy of Calgary, and the population were evidently much pleased that "he had got religion, and was going right ahead into better ways," as my next neighbour said to me.

Ted made a rattling speech, in which he appealed very pointedly to some old pals in the hall to come up to the penitent form, and was launching out into somewhat minute details of his past life, when the captain put both hands on his shoulders, wheeled him round into his seat, and told him his was "an experience that had better be taken in sections, and they would have some more tomorrow night." I conversed with several of the audience coming out, and they all spoke in the warmest terms of the officers of the Army in Calgary, and it would evidently fare ill with any cowboy or idler who ventured to say a rude word to any of the hallelujah lasses" [*A Trip Round the World 1887-8* (1888): 65-66].

The three females who "opened" the Calgary Corps—Captain Helen Mercer and Lieutenants Patterson and Iverach—were by no means an anomaly. Across Canada, female officers were storming the nation's so-called "forts of darkness" as aggressively and as effectively (some say more effectively) than their male counterparts.

In Ingersoll, Ont., on June 23, 1883, Captain Annie O'Leary and Lieutenant Woodyard "took the town by storm," reported the *Chronicle;* in Belleville, Ont., on September 23 of the same year "the streets were thronged, and in the Metropolitan Hall there was not standing room left" as Captain Nellie Ryerson and Lieutenant Emma Churchill, assisted by the effervescent Captain Abbie Thompson from Kingston, Ont., drew most of the townspeople into their makeshift barracks. The same Emma Churchill, who had opened the corps in Guelph, Ont., was to be found, in late 1885, in her hometown of

Portugal Cove, N.L., where (though on her honeymoon) she could not refrain from "spreading the gospel message," thereby introducing Salvationism to the island colony. When the Army officially opened there in January 1886, it was four young females—Captains Mary Ann Collins, Maggie Phillips and Lena Kimmerley, and Cadet Alice Larder—who braved the snowballs of the St. John's urchins to hold their open-air meetings on Barter's Hill, commencing what would become the most exuberant brand of Salvationism in the Army world.

In the West, it was nearly always two or three female officers who invaded the new towns—Captain Mary Hackett in Winnipeg, Victoria and Vancouver. And later, in Edmonton, Captain Marie Kadey and Lieutenant Hattie Scott arrived by themselves on July 6, 1893—11 years before the town became incorporated and 12 before Alberta became a province of Canada. They became the town's new sensation, for, though many may have heard of the Army, few people had seen it in the flesh, especially with such beautiful faces as Kadey and Scott, dressed as they were in their tight-fitting blue-black dresses and large poke bonnets. Soon they were walking the streets with their bundle of *War Cry*s, enchanting everyone they met (especially the editor of the *Bulletin*), and filling the little Methodist Church, which they had rented, to its fullest capacity.

As we peruse the pages of the early Canadian *War Cry* we see their names and their stories, as they went into towns (usually in pairs) and sometimes braved unfriendly receptions, sang their songs and prayed in the market squares, went about securing a place in which to worship and then tried to convince people of their need of salvation. Tessie Hall, Annie Hassen, Eliza Wood, Minnie Leidy, Mattie Calhoun, Ida Russell, Ada Hind, Eliza Crosby, Grace Hill, Annie Teagle, Ella Smith, Maggie Barker, Aggie Cowan, Blanche Goodall, Bella Nunn, Nellie Banks, and many, many more: most of whom remained relatively unknown, but a few of whom became minor celebrities in their time.

Take Captain Abigail Thompson, for example. When she arrived in Kingston, Ont., from the United States on January 29, 1883, the town was changed forever. At first, as the Kingston *Whig* reported the "opening foray," it seemed a fairly normal Salvation Army invasion:

About 10:30 yesterday morning those passing and residing in the vicinity of Market Square were attracted by a vocal chorus, rendered by a quartette of persons. Pedestrians halted, listened, and drew near. Windows were raised, and a number of heads appeared. The music continued: it was undoubtedly attractive, and one by one the audience swelled until in groups two or three hundred persons had assembled. The singers were evidently peace-makers, their demonstration was of a friendly, solicitous character: their mission was quite apparent as they knelt upon the snow and engaged in prayer. Thus did The Salvation Army attack this city.

But when Captain Abby (as she was soon called) began the battle in earnest, she startled the whole town. She was, said the *Whig*, "the brightest little evangelist Kingston has ever seen," and when she held her first meetings in the Victoria Music Hall, "every seat was occupied, the lobby was jammed, the stairs were blocked up, and four or five hundred people got no further than the door." She was not only strikingly beautiful, in her long, tight-fitting Army uniform, but she was a brilliant speaker, known for her "quaint sayings," her vivacious personality and her platform oratory. So popular did she become that when the first barracks was erected on Queen and Bagot Streets, it became known as "Abby Temple." A soap manufacturer named one of his popular brands of soap after the Army captain, calling it "Abby Soap," a prominent citizen named his yacht "Captain Abby," and, shortly after her term was over, a small biography was published extolling her brilliance (unfortunately, no copy survives).

There were many prominent Kingstonians who were drawn to Captain Abby and The Salvation Army, discrediting the view that all her converts were drawn from the lower classes. One of the Army's noteworthy supporters was Agnes Maule Machar, the noted poet and journalist and an avid advocate of female rights and temperance. She not only attended Army meetings in Kingston but wrote an able defense of the Army called *Red Cross Knights of The Salvation Army* in which she provides excellent descriptions of its early work.

Another noted—or perhaps notorious—Army acolyte was Dr.

Henry Wilson, a leading churchman, who had been assistant priest at St. George's cathedral for 16 years. He became enamoured of the Army when Captain Abby was there, attended Army meetings (even speaking at them) and, by becoming more charismatic in his preaching, was censured by the church authorities. When he claimed to have experienced "conversion" at an Army meeting, those authorities ordered him to take a three-month leave, a condition of his return being "to sever all relations with the Army." But Dr. Wilson believed in his conversion, and so stayed in New York where he became an assistant in another St. George's church while continuing his support of and close association with the Army.

But Machar and Wilson were not the only socially prominent people to become enamoured of Captain Abby. Perhaps the most prominent, and indeed the most controversial, was the prime minister of Canada himself, Sir John A. Macdonald. In 1883, the 68-year-old nation's patriarch sat in on Captain Abby's "hallelujah" sermons three nights in a row. The *Whig* reported that "the jam was something awful. People collected at the front of City Hall (where she had been holding her meetings) at 6 o'clock, and five minutes after the doors were opened the hall was half-filled. When Abby was reading the Scripture lesson, Sir John appeared. He had arrived at the hall late and, after standing at the door for a few moments, was invited in by an Army sergeant. As he walked up the aisle people craned their necks and acted as if they had never seen him before. Captain Abby stopped reading and remarked, "Now, don't make a fuss. He's only a gentleman and you all know him. If I dared I'd ask him on the platform and then your faces would be turned this way. Just give me your attention!" A moment later she closed her Bible and remarked, "I was just thinking that if the Lord had appeared as suddenly as that gentleman, there would be more noise and confusion, and not many smiling faces!" Then she proceeded to exhort people to live so that they would be glad instead of afraid at the Second Coming of the Saviour. What Sir John thought of those boisterous meetings we do not know (though they may have been no more boisterous than some sessions of Parliament). We only know what the newspapers thought. The Kingston *Whig* regretted (with obvious irony) that the prime minister chose not "to give his experience of salvation" and stated (with no seeming irony at all) that he was much concerned about Captain Abby's health:

> Sir John remarked to a friend last evening that Captain Abby was straining her voice, and that she would have to spare herself some, indeed take a long rest, or she would be afflicted with bronchitis. She was too valuable a little woman, he said, to be thus incapacitated. Two days later the *Whig* reported that Captain Abby had visited Sir John and had induced him to subscribe $25 towards the barracks now in the course of erection. He told the captain he was interested in her labours and invited her to Ottawa to spend with him any holidays she desired. He attended the holiness meeting and soldiers' roll-call last night and remained there throughout the evening. He augmented the collection by a crisp bank note.

Sir John A. Macdonald's attraction to The Salvation Army (or, per-haps, more likely to Captain Abby herself) was a circumstance so strange and so seemingly self-serving that most newspapers just laughed it off—much as they had already laughed off the "devil-scar-ing" tactics of the Army itself. They dismissed his admiration of the "Hallelujah Lass" as either an old man's infatuation or as a seasoned politician's sly attempt to gain votes. They leaned towards the latter view. Though they all agreed that if Sir John were ever to reach heaven, he would have to do it via the Army route which, they said, was this: "If you can't get in at the Golden Gate, climb over the garden wall."

The Toronto *Evening News* posed the question, "Now suppose Sir John should be converted, would his sins be forgiven?" Without answering such a theologically loaded question, the newspaper went on to suggest that the "wily statesman just wants to make a good impression on the Kingstonians who are crazy over The Salvation Army. If Sir John was to represent the limestone city again he is pursing a wily policy."

The Toronto *Telegram* had a different slant on Sir John's interest in Salvationism:

> As he has frequently expressed a desire to have hen's wings attached to his spinal column and become an angel, so that he may look down upon the Canadian Pacific trains speeding across the continent, it is likely that when the Army goes to Ottawa he will become one of its most enthusiastic admirers.

Supporting the view that Sir John was attending Army meetings simply to gain public sympathy is the fact that at the moment of his infatuation he was being charged with bribery in the recent election in Napanee, Ont., and on October 13, 1883, was unseated in that district. "When people get into trouble," ventured the Kingston *Whig*, "they generally seek the consolation of religion. This accounts for the attendance of Sir John Macdonald at the Salvation Army meetings before the election trial in Napanee." The Toronto *Globe* maliciously stated that a week earlier Sir John had joined the Army under the name of "Happy Jack" and a few days later was unseated for bribery and corruption. "Such a fall from grace," it gleefully suggested, "is seldom recorded."

There seems to be no other explanation of Sir John's visits to The Salvation Army than to say he was, in a sense, infatuated with Captain Abby. Not so much with her as a woman, perhaps, but as a powerful speaker and charismatic personality. So captivated was he that rumour suggested he had offered her the chaplaincy of the

Senate in Ottawa. But, after Captain Abby left Kingston in November, though Sir John remained a friend of the Army, he did not again attend one of its meetings. As for the captain, she returned to the United States (from which she had come) and later married an Army officer of the same name, becoming Mrs. Captain Thompson. No doubt the story of her friendship with Canada's prime minister was often repeated to her children. It certainly was in Army circles for a long time. Sir John's visits to the Army were often held up as testimony to the fact that William Booth's "Blood-and-Fire" mission appealed not just to the low-born but to men and women of high estate as well. More likely, however, they were a testimony to the power of the female preacher in an age when such a thing was both a novelty and a decided attraction.

An attraction, one might say, which did not please everybody, especially clergy of the "old school." The Reverend Andrew Wilson, for example, a leading clergyman in Kingston during Abby Thompson's officership there, offered this comment, which fairly summed up the views of many others of his persuasion:

In this Army, so far as its officers and exercises are concerned, there is neither male nor female, all are one and the same. It is nothing to them that God has enjoined, by his inspired apostle, "Let the women learn in silence, with all subjection; but I suffer not a woman to teach, nor to usurp authority over the man, but to be in silence. For Adam was first formed, then Eve, and Adam was not deceived, but the woman being deceived was in the transgression"—1 Timothy 2:11. Also, in his first epistle to the Corinthians, 14th chapter, "Let your women keep silence in the churches; for it is not permitted unto them to speak, but they are commanded to be under obedience, as also saith the law. And if they will learn anything, let them ask their husbands at home; for it a shame for a woman to speak in the church." The reasons given for these strong injunctions are as cogent today as when they were first penned. Yet in the Army women are made lieutenants and captains, to preside over and command the Army's corps. This practice is not only inconsistent with the position in which it has pleased God to place women, but, also, with that modesty which is such an ornament to her sex" [*The Salvation Army: Its Government and Practices* (1884): 17].

To such specious arguments, Catherine Booth, who championed a female ministry, had already supplied a cogent rebuttal. In her pamphlet titled *Female Ministry,* published many years earlier, she had effectively dealt with such criticisms as those put forward by Wilson, saying in part:

Why should woman be confined exclusively to the kitchen and the distaff, any more than man to the field or workshop? Did not God, and has not nature, assigned to man *his* sphere of labour, "to till the ground and to dress it?" And, if exemption is claimed from this kind of toil for a portion of the male sex, on the ground of their possessing ability for intellectual and moral pursuits, we must be allowed to claim the same privilege for women; nor can we see the exception more *unnatural* in the one case than the other, or why God in this solitary instance has endowed a being with powers which he never intended her to employ.

It was, in fact, largely through Catherine's commitment, that William, her husband, enshrined female equality in the Army's charters. In his *Orders and Regulations for Field Officers* (1885) he stated that "The Army refuses to make any difference between men and women as to rank, authority and duties, but opens the highest positions to women as well as to men." Though, as several historians have pointed out, it was the male officers, not the female, who gained the "highest positions" (most leadership positions in Canada were held by men), it is reasonable to suggest that many women who otherwise would never in the ordinary sense have been given an opportunity to excel were given one by The Salvation Army. Of course, the Army benefited greatly from their devotion and appeal. Given their powers of persuasion with male audiences, their reminders of mothers and sisters "back home," and their acknowledged ability to preach with passion—their participation in the Army's advancement was a stroke of genius which reaped huge benefits for the young religious movement.

THREE

Going Deep into the Community

Early Salvationists as Practical Evangelists

Y OU MIGHT," SAID ONE OBSERVER, "BE ANNOYED WITH, OR even opposed to, the Army's noisy street meetings, but how can you be anything but approving of their determination to reach into the lowest places to help people in need and bring them the message of the gospel?" It was a sentiment echoed throughout Canada in the 1880s, and one which eventually persuaded most Canadians that The Salvation Army was indeed a valuable community asset, drums and tambourines notwithstanding. For it soon became evident that Salvationists were not content merely to sing and preach, nor only to march in the streets, but were prepared to offer practical assistance in the remotest corners of their communities. Long before William Booth launched his social wing in 1891, they were seeking out the poor in the slums, visiting the taverns and jails, supplying meals to the poor, and generally becoming "the Army of the helping hand"—all as a means of promoting the gospel.

In the slums, especially. Many corps had visitation brigades whose purpose it was to "visit from house to house, pray with the people, and, where possible, relieve their wants, help them make their houses clean and tidy, and try to educate them to habits of neatness, acting on the principle of cleanliness being next to Godliness." In Toronto there were six such brigades, one for each of the districts of the city. Talking to a reporter from the Toronto *Globe* in 1887, one of those Salvationists had the following to say:

My corps have gone to as many as 30 houses in one day, and I never before had any idea of what poverty was. People have no idea of it! They don't dream of the extent of the suffering that there is now right beside them in the city! About two weeks ago I noticed a young girl at one of our meetings. In speaking to her I found she was in deep distress. I asked her where she lived. She did not want to tell me at first. I said, "Do you live with your mother?"

"My mother lives in the country, a long way from here," she replied.

"Have you been in service here?" said I.

"I was, but I have lost my place. I cannot get employment. I have no money to pay my board or to pay my way home to my mother."

I could see that she was desperate and from the way she spoke those last words I knew that she had made up her mind to go upon the streets. I had some little money then, which was given to me by Mr. Gooderham, and I paid her fare home. She went straight off on the midnight train, giving one of our soldiers the keys of her room to get her trunk, which we sent on the next day. We have since received a postcard thanking us, and stating that she had arrived home all right. I think there was a soul saved there.

The stories continued:

Some time ago a gentleman who kept a store on Yonge Street failed in business. He had a wife but no children. They had hitherto had a good, comfortable home, but everything was sold out by the creditors. The man could not find employment of any kind, and became distracted, and took to drink, although he had never drunk before. He left his wife and obtained employment around one of the hotels in the city, but he hides from his wife so that she cannot see him, because he is ashamed to meet her. He never gave her anything to contribute to her support, and she was left destitute. Being a clever needlewoman she obtained some fancy needlework to do. She rented a little room at a dollar and a half a month. And managed to keep herself from starving for six weeks, but the scanty pittance she got for her needlework, while it kept her in bread, was not sufficient to pay the rent, and she owed for one month. About two weeks ago the lady who employed her decided that she no longer needed her services, and her condition was now worse than before. The landlady asked her to pay up her rent, threatening that if she did pay it up she would have to go out. The poor woman begged to be allowed to stay, and said she would go and try to borrow the money to pay it that night. She came to see us, but we had no money to give her. She was afraid to face the landlady, and that night, a bitterly cold night, she slept in the woodshed. Since that she has several times slept out in the streets. She would have slept out in the street last night had not one of our soldiers taken her home to his house [*The War Cry*, January 15, 1887].

It was soon known that Salvationists would do all in their power to help the down-and-out. "The other day," an officer told a *Globe* reporter, "I received a list of names which was sent to me by the mayor with a request I should look up these cases and see what I could do for them. I visited these people and in nearly every case found that the difficulty was poverty pure and simple. They were in extreme destitution, which could not be said to be through drink, and was not the result of their own doing, but was caused by their inability to get work. They asked me what I came for, and when I spoke about their souls they said, 'Oh, we have our church, but we want food.' " And it was the Army's growing reputation as an agency willing to supply such wants which made such people as the mayor and Mr. Gooderham, the Toronto philanthropist, support their efforts.

And then there were the local jails to be visited. Take London, Ont., for example—a town where they not only locked up Salvationists who "beat drums" in their streets but where they, ironically it seems, also allowed Salvationists to visit the jails and hold brief meetings for the inmates.

It was Sunday, February 18, 1883. The local jail was rather quiet this Sunday morning, with only 10 people in the cells, most of them awaiting misdemeanour charges after a Saturday night of carousing. A nice time to put one's feet up thought Turnkey Kelly. But his heels had hardly hit the top of his desk, and his chair barely tilted, before the sound of singing brought him fully upright. And before he had recovered his wits there they were, a band of Salvationists at the door of the jail, waiting to be admitted, to hold, they said, a short religious service for the inmates. Out of surprise as much as goodwill (especially since they were accompanied by a reporter from the *Advertiser*), Kelly admitted them, listened and watched as they sang hymns, read a portion of Scripture, said a few prayers and talked with those in the cells. After 15 minutes, they thanked the turnkey, and marched back to their barracks, but, wrote the reporter next day, "it is understood that they intend visiting that institution weekly hereafter."

Very soon almost every corps in the new Canadian Territory had emulated London's initiative and were "bombarding" the local jails ("bombarding" being a term Salvationists liked to use). In Hamilton, Ont., Sunday morning services were begun at the Barton Street jail "to the satisfaction of the prisoners. Hallelujah Bertha presented the prisoners with 25 *War Cry*s. Many of the soldiers also put papers into their hands as the Army marched out of the grounds singing a salvation hymn. Captain Eastwood's address to the prisoners was very effective" [*Spectator*, April 14, 1884]. And as far away as Yarmouth, N.S., there were Salvationists (with good singing and speaking voices) ready to do what they called "jail duty":

Shortly after the Army opened here, meetings were started in [the jail], and have been kept up two weekly ever since.... At first the meetings were poorly attended, only a few soldiers and converts would gather, but God was there to own and bless their labours; it has since grown until the whole alleyway in front of the cells is crowded. There have been 15 prisoners in during this time, eight of which are in at present, every one of the number having professed conversion.... Now this is grand, and just the kind of work that will make all heaven rejoice; but it has not ended here, the fame of these meetings has gone abroad, and many have come to see for themselves, some through curiosity, some by invitation, and the result has been more souls saved. The meetings are not led by the officers but mostly by Brother Sleith and Brother Bryant. May the great God of power prosper this grand and glorious work, and help our dear comrades to lead these poor fallen creatures from darkness to light [*The War Cry*, June 30, 1888].

Those early services in the local jails were not, as James Tack-aberry notes in his extensive research, "in any way, part of an organized ministry in corrections; they were not ordered by head-quarters, rather they were the outcome of the zeal of the pioneer Salvationists to reach those who were the outcasts of society, those who were hurting. The soldiers were heeding the call of Christ to visit those in prison, as recorded in the 25th chapter of the Gospel according to Saint Matthew" [*Correctional and Justice Services* (1994), p. 6]. They were, in other words, a response to William Booth's injunction to "*go to*" the people with the gospel—to put their religion into action, not merely when people came for help, but seeking them out in the jails and slums. And in the very place Salvationists most despised— the pub or (as most Canadians termed it) the tavern.

Perhaps the most iconic activity of early Salvationists—one continued well into the 20th century—was what the Salvationists called "*War Cry* booming." As a practical effort, selling *War Cry*s at the town's various business establishments, and often door-to-door in the neighbourhood (many to non-Army regular customers), and, most particularly, in the pubs and taverns, often netted the officers most of their weekly income. For people, especially in the pubs, often gave more than what the paper nominally sold for. But "*War Cry* booming" was also a sure means of introducing people to the gospel, an occasion for prayer and counselling, and a way to invite people to the Army barracks.

It was one of the Army's most profitable means of evangelism. And, surprisingly, was welcomed not only in the businesses and homes, but in the pubs as well. Describing her term in Montreal in 1884, Captain Hattie Yerex tells of how the notorious saloon-keeper, Charles McKiernan, otherwise known as Joe Beef, always "received them kindly, and bought all the *War Cry*s we had, whether few or many. Then he would say, 'You must sing and pray with the men. You know they need it badly. I can feed their bodies, but can do nothing for their souls'; and no matter how rough or drunk they were, a word or look from him was enough to secure quietness while we stood in their midst (perhaps with a monkey pulling at our dress) and talked and sang of Jesus and his love. And many a pair of wet eyes I have seen as we have gone on our knees to pray" [*The War Cry*, February 4, 1893].

Salvationists seem to have been received with as much grace by so many other publicans (was it mere kindness or a bit of daring?) that the most popular picture of Army activity—in stories, cartoons and poems—was that of the hallelujah lass proffering her *War Cry* to an habitué of the local bar. John Wilson Bengough, the well-known editor of the Toronto satirical magazine, *Grip*, and a staunch supporter of the Army, wrote a very popular poem on that very subject, called "The War Cry":

In the elegant rotunda of a fine up-town hotel
(A favourite lounge of tourist, commercial man and swell),
In little knots and circles, in coteries and sets,
The idlers chatted gaily and enjoyed their cigarettes.

A drummer from Kentucky (in the wine and liquor trade)
His stock of brand new stories to a genial group displayed,
And bursts of merry laughter acclaimed each happy hit,
Like thunder-peals responding to his lightning flash of wit.

Within the vaulted entry and across the polished tiles
To'rds the group of flippant gossips, under fire of rakish smiles,
Came a pair of mild-faced maidens, clad in modest navy blue,
With scoop-bonnets of the Army and the badge of crimson hue;

And with gentle step approaching, as the loungers stood at ease,
Spoke in accents low and winning: "Will you buy a *War Cry*, please?"
Offering a sample of the paper from the bundle that each bore,
"Will you please to buy a copy?—It will tell you of the war."

"Bless my soul!" exclaimed the drummer, with an air of mock alarm,
Putting on his gold-rimmed *pince nez*—"a *War Cry*, little marm?

Why, I thought the war was over and ended long ere this—
Been another Indian slaughter? Or what's the matter, miss?"

A smile went round the circle at this clever, ready jest,
And the hand that held the paper trembled as it fell to rest;
But upon the jester's features the lass's eyes were set,
The sweetest yet the saddest eyes his glance had ever met.

"No," she said, in earnest, quav'ring tones, and tears were in
her voice,
"The war is not yet over, nor the time come to rejoice;
With dead and dying comrades the trenches yet are filled,
And the field is strewn with victims—but not by Indians
killed.

"'Tis sinful human passion, the lust and greed of gold,
That slaughters these our brothers today in hosts untold—
That slays them not with bullets, but with ardent spirits fell,
With wine, and beer, and whiskey, the artillery of hell.

"Oh, sir, are *you* a helper in this awful work of woe?
Do eyes of murdered babies glare icily at *you*?
Do ghosts of famished mothers and wraiths of ruined sons
Cry from the tomb for vengeance on you, who man the guns?

May God forbid! But, oh, sir! This long and weary fight
Is raging all about us—nor ceases day and night—
And you, who praise the soldier who faces shot and shell,
Have you no manly honour for us who fight as well?

"Think you 'tis any pleasure that we, two puny girls,
Should go where laughter greets us or the lip of scorner curls?
Nay; but our Master's colours we dare to hold aloft,
And bear, as once he bore for us, the taunts of those who
scoffed.

"'Tis for your souls we labour; we do not prize your gold;

But oh, don't slight our Master; his love can ne'er be told.
You do not mean to be unkind, your hearts are not all bad,
But your thoughtless mirth makes sadder our hearts already
sad!"

No man in all that circle now bore a leering smile,
But moistened eyes were fixed upon that face so free of guile;
And the jester whispered softly, his manner ill at ease,
Said huskily, "God bless you! Sell me a *War Cry*, please."

Perhaps as iconic as the *"War Cry* boomer" is The Salvation Army's Christmas kettle. Indeed, The Salvation Army and Christmas is an association most Canadians still rely on—the Army's kettles, hampers and Christmas dinners have become for many Canadians key symbols of the Christmas season. It has long been that way. It was for the Army an extension of its motto, "With Heart to God and Hand to Man," and was a yet another means of assuring the public that its mission was a practical as well as a soul-saving one.

Just which corps was the first to sponsor a "Christmas dinner for the poor" is a matter of some dispute, but certain it is that, from as early as the 1880s, the poor were being treated to what was then called a "Christmas Carnival." In the Montreal *Witness* of December 27, 1888, for example, we find the following vivid description:

"Christmas comes but once a year, and when it comes it brings good cheer." Montreal can, unhappily, boast of a considerable number of "the great unfed" who have been unable to share in the season's festivities. With a view to providing a good meal to those who through want of employment or distressed circumstances were unable to make any provision for the Christmas celebration, The Salvation Army made an appeal to the public for funds for this purpose through the *Witness*, and a very generous response was made both in money and in kind. Invitations were distributed throughout the haunts of poverty in the city, with as much caution as possible without being too particular, and last night the Army barracks in St. Alexander

Street presented a scene of gaiety and animation that would have delighted the heart of the veriest curmudgeon. Nearly a thousand men, women and children were at the feast, and in relays of a hundred were regaled with a substantial meal of roast beef and mutton, turkey, hams, plum puddings, mince pies, cakes, fruit, and tea and coffee, to which they did most ample justice. To give some idea of the provision made it may be stated that the Army larder contained 800 pounds of beef and mutton, 18 turkeys, eight hams, 700 mince pies, and 250 packets of candy for the little ones. There was a willing staff of helpers, who amply supplied the wants of their guests, and during the progress of dinner some excellent selections of vocal and instrumental music was agreeably discoursed by a number of ladies and gentlemen who had been invited to attend.

After dinner a monster procession was formed and headed by the brass band, bearing torch-lights, some of the principal streets were paraded to the stirring strains of the Army band. The service afterwards held in the barracks was of a bright and cheering character, and was rendered additionally interesting by the addresses of several prominent gentlemen in the city. Major Spooner was in command, and after the usual devotional exercises had been conducted with characteristic vigour, he delivered a short but forcible address of welcome, and subsequently stated that towards the expenses of the dinner he had received about $201 in money, and contributions of 150 pounds of meat; but the expenditure had exceeded that amount by some $12 or $13, which he hoped to clear off by the evening's collection. They had, however, enough food left to feed 500 people, and, amid loud cheering, he cordially invited the men to a second dinner on Friday evening and to bring their wives and children with them.... It is proposed at Friday's gathering to distribute a quantity of cast-off clothing, which has been sent in for the benefit of the most destitute.

Each Christmas thereafter, in most cities throughout Canada, The Salvation Army provided a Christmas dinner for the "deserving poor." In Toronto, as another example, in 1892, an elaborate festivity called "A Juvenile Feast," intended for children only, caught the attention of the city's newspapers, as more than 800 children crowded into the auditorium of the Salvation Army Temple on Albert Street, to be fed and entertained (Christian style, of course). Here is how *The War Cry* (January 7, 1893), described the occasion:

Now everyone ought to know by this time, that the little ones of Canada share a very warm corner in Mrs. Cornelie Booth's heart. But it was only one week before Christmas that she decided that children must have a Christmas tree, and a banquet, to gladden their hearts and bring little sunshine into their lives, in the midst of the cold and snow of the dark winter days.

So, with the assistance of Brigadier Holland, and Staff-Captain Friedrich, Ensign Archibald, and others of the staff, whose hearts are full of love for the suffering children, the city was canvassed, appeals were written to the daily papers, and provisions were collected.

With open-hearted generosity, almost everyone responded. Some with gifts of money, some with food, some with presents. Some gave bags of nuts, some almonds—everything, in fact—raisins, figs, candies, tea, fruit, "sugar and spice, and all that's nice."

The tickets were printed, the children invited, and the day arrived.

Down the streets in every direction eager-faced little ones came pouring along, and into the big Temple; boys and girls, big and little, clean and dirty, helter-skelter, and pell-mell, and there before their delighted eyes stood the Christmas tree—but *such* a Christmas tree!

It looked as though a piece of the forest had been carted wholesale home and planted on the platform, nearly 50 feet high. The whole undertaking, beyond all question, had been beautifully arranged, especially taking into consideration that the whole thing had been crowded into a few day's doing.

The great, green tree reached almost to the ceiling, and its branches were covered with beauty and laden with fruit. Gold and silver threads were thickly interwoven like glittering cob-webs, and snowy wool whitened the boughs like hoar frost; nearly a hundred candles glittered and gleamed with little lights, and a multitude of Chinese lanterns were slung up around the galleries.

To say the children were astonished is nothing—they were almost intoxicated with excitement—wild with delight!

On either side of the tree, the tables for the tea—no, the feast—were arranged, rising tier above tier around, covered with clean white linen, and loaded with good things.

Then the children came, and they came, and they came; and not one was turned away for want of a ticket. Whilst one dear brother brought a van with a pair of horses, and kept coming and going down the streets, returning each time with a load of joyous little guests, and the babies—oh, yes, of course, the big ones brought the little ones, and there was no lack even for the babies. Still it was found there was room, and a brother with a big bell went out into the highways and hedges to fetch the forgotten or unknown.

Then they feasted—and they *did* feast! It was no wonder they got excited—who wouldn't under such circumstances?

At last that tea was over, positively finished, except for the remains that were stuffed into pockets to be taken home to be finished and shared with someone else—mother and baby, perhaps.

The banquet done, the lights were lowered, and the lovely limelight was made to play with different colours on the waiting Christmas tree.

Semi-darkness prevailed, but the children were too much overwhelmed with excitement to listen much to the poverty of mere words, except when Mrs. Booth talked to them, and told them stories about other boys and girls, and talked to them of the first Christmas Day, and the Baby Jesus cradled in a manger; who became poor that they might be rich. Very quietly indeed they listened whilst she pleaded with them to try and be like Jesus too, to show Him that they loved him by being good and obedient to their parents, and teachers, and playmates. Very lustily they responded when she asked all those who meant to try to do right to raise their hands, and fix bayonets, and fire a volley.

Then they sang, no difficulty about *that*—sang with might and main, sang with heart and soul, or at any rate with the full force of their lusty little lungs, sang—

"Then we'll lift up the banner on high,"

and each one of the 800 congregation raised and flourished a bright flag with the Canadian ensign stamped on it. That was delightful, at least the children seemed to think it was, and so did Mrs. Booth as you could judge by the expression on her face as she placed in each hand a package of nuts, and candies, and figs, and fruit, as the homeward-bound crowd passed by her to the door.

The Toronto newspapers—the *Empire,* the *Mail* and the *World*—were lavish in their praise of the Army's effort. As one put it, "Volley after volley of hurrahs rent the air, as the children were sent to their homes to dream of Santa Claus and The Salvation Army." And, as those newspapers rightly concluded, The Salvation Army worked on the principle that "faith without works is dead, and while they observe the former they do not forget the latter."

It is well known, of course, that some of those initiatives eventually became the responsibility of the Army's social wing. In the jails, for example, though non-officer Salvationists continued to visit, the Army was, by 1890, assigning officers to the work—to meet prisoners as they were discharged, to house them in the new Prison Gate Homes, and to administer a system of parole for the Canadian government. The Army's correctional and justice services department became an essential part of its professionally administered social outreach program. Similarly, slum rescue work—in the form of "gutter and garret brigades", rescue homes, hostels and rehabilitation centres, children's homes and Christmas dinners were all eventually effectively administered by trained officers as part of the Army's social services.

In the beginning, however, all these attempts to reach more deeply into the community were the result of corps initiatives. Those early lay Salvationists who visited the jails and homes of the poor, who went into the slums to help in practical ways to better people's lives, were doing so simply because they believed their Christian commitment required it of them. And, by doing so, they established a public trust which enabled the Army to later gain access to the jails and the slums on a permanent basis. It all began, we might say, because ordinary Salvationists believed it was their duty to take the gospel to the people, wherever they might be located.

And, in a very important sense, the work of visitation—of poor homes, hospitals and, in many cases, Salvation Army social institutions—was assumed for many years (and still is to a certain extent) by lay Salvationists. In 1893, in fact, Herbert Booth, the Canadian

commander, decided (at the prompting of his wife, Cornelie, said some) to officially recognize those lay people already engaged in social outreach (visiting jails and pubs, for example) and attempt to enlarge the work by creating what he called a league of mercy, similar to that which Commissioner Coombs had already established in Australia.

"By these sisters of salvation," wrote Herbert in 1893 (ignoring the fact that some men were also involved), "the hospitals are visited, the prisons are prayed in, the sick tended, and the slums gospelled. But the time has come for development. It is a shame, that with such facilities as are offered us, we should delay. Scarcely a prison or hospital in Protestant Canada is closed against our agents, and where there are hindrances, they could, with push and patience, be removed. So we propose to organize the league from the centre. A secretary is to be appointed to Mrs. Booth for this purpose, and branches of the league of mercy may soon be expected in such cities as London, Hamilton, Peterboro', Montreal, Kingston, Saint John, Halifax, Victoria, and Winnipeg. The league of mercy will grow up alongside our social work." It was, in fact, Herbert Booth's intention that the league would be the link between the corps and the social institution. Its members would not only, as they had done, visit the hospitals, but provide personal contact with the "inmates" of the social institutions and facilitate, if willing, their entry into the corps as possible Salvationists.

Just before Herbert Booth left Canada in 1896, he appointed Blanche Read superintendent of the rescue work in Canada and included in her supervision the league of mercy. Mrs. Read was, as her biographer notes, well qualified for the position, having been in charge of the Home for Inebriate Women in Toronto and having opened several rescues homes in St. John's, N.L., Halifax and Winnipeg. She was also ideal in that her passion for the work was so obvious, and her eloquence so compelling, in the many speeches she gave across the country promoting the rescue mission. She was both dedicated and tireless.

Soon, leagues of mercy were commenced in nearly every corps she visited from St. John's, N.L., to Victoria. She designed for them a unique badge—a red cross upon a white enamelled button (later changed to a white cross on a red background) with the words "League of Mercy: Inasmuch."

"Some called them," writes Mary Morgan Dean, "the women with the cross on their arm and the cross in their hearts." They carried comfort, cheer, music, flowers, little dainties and uplifting literature into hospitals, old people's homes, poor houses, asylums, and the homes in distress, bereavement and poverty" [*The Lady with the Other Lamp* (1919), p. 188]. And, during the First World War, the league was especially busy, and spiritually effective, visiting the families of soldiers overseas.

The kind of league of mercy visitation described by Mrs. Read was typical of most, and one which even members today can readily appreciate. Mary Morgan Dean wrote:

> While Mrs. Read was having one of her campaign inspections of all the work, she was invited to visit [the old people's home in Montreal]. Whenever permitted, she always took some musicians to a meeting of this kind and on this occasion an orchestra of stringed instruments accompanied her—violin, mandolin and guitar—the music delighted the old people. Hundreds of them were gathered in their assembly hall, in wheeled chairs, on sofas, on crutches, helped, when lame, by friends and attendants, and those who could not leave their beds were able at least to enjoy the singing.
>
> They asked for some of the old songs of long ago, which were heartily given, as well as bright and happy new ones. Mrs. Read's experience over and over again was that music was of the greatest assistance in breaking down prejudice, softening hearts that appeared hard as adamant, and overcoming obstacles in sin-charted minds; when some "old sweet song" brought a rush of memories of happy childhood. To those whose childhood had no happy memories—too frequently the case—the power of music, skilfully rendered, often plays on some forgotten emotion, some moment of desire for higher things in sub-consciousness, and the spirit is caught by some statement of hope [*The Lady with the Other Lamp* (1919), pp. 190-191].

In the early years, then, the ordinary Salvationist was not only actively involved in the evangelical activities of his or her corps, but was often quite involved in many forms of social outreach for evangelical purposes. Slum brigades, visitation of the sick, meetings in the local jails, pub-booming on a Saturday evening, were all, in varying degrees, responsibilities of the lay Salvationists. Though this kind of activity lessened when the Army became actively involved in social work, league of mercy work, jail visitation and pub-booming remained important avenues of practical outreach for many years to come.

FOUR

Salvation Army Mountaineers

Evangelizing the Interior of British Columbia

W HEN WILLIAM BOOTH AMBITIOUSLY ORDERED HIS salvation soldiers to "go to the people with the gospel," he was living in London, England, one of the densest and most-crowded cities in the world. It was, in that context, an easy order to carry out. The people were nearly all within easy reach. And even in the smaller cities of Canada—in Toronto, Hamilton, Ont.,Vancouver or Halifax—when his Salvationists embraced that principle, as they most certainly did, the jails and the pubs, and even the burgeoning slums were very close to the doorsteps of their barracks.

But, in the rugged and almost-inaccessible mountains of British Columbia? That seemed to be another matter altogether.

Or was it?

Thomas Coombs, the young commissioner of the Canadian Territory, did not think so. In late 1887, just a few months after the Army had planted its flag in Western Canada, he called for volunteers to serve as "outriders" in the interior of British Columbia—to visit the scattered miners, lumbermen and ranchers along the Fraser River, along the lower Thompson, and into the Nicola Valley. With headquarters at Kamloops, they were to ride west and south to such places as Nicola and Douglas Lake Ranch, then to Lytton, until they turned north to visit Spence's Bridge, Lillooet, Clinton, Dog Creek, Alkali Lake, 150 Mile House, Williams Lake and as far north as Soda Creek.

It was an ambitious venture, and many people must have thought that Commissioner Coombs, fresh out from England, had no idea of the immensity of the country or the seemingly insuperable obstacles in the way of evangelistic outreach. Others might have insinuated (or even openly declared) that all Booth's soldiers seemed a little crazy anyway, and nothing they tried would surprise them. But the Salvationists themselves firmly believed that where there was a will—and The Salvation Army had already shown that it had one—there would be a way. And, in their many imaginative efforts at evangelization, they had proved that to be so.

In the summer of 1890, then, and for approximately three years after, Salvation Army officers on horseback—men like Captains George Arkett and Robert Smith, Lieutenants Jarvis and Cromartey—followed the routes the gold-seekers had taken many years before and engaged in an itinerant kind of Salvationism aimed at making contact with the lonely miners and ranchers of British Columbia.

"Gold is precious," wrote Captain Smith. "That is why there is so much risk and labour attached to it. The same with soul-saving among the Cascade Mountains in British Columbia. Souls are precious, but hard to get them into the kingdom of God."

On his first foray as a Salvation mountaineer, Smith left Kamloops on August 6, 1890, arriving the next morning at Spence's Bridge. There, while waiting to purchase a horse and supplies, he assisted Rev. Murray, the Methodist minister, in his services. There were, he wrote, "about 40 [Indians] present and a few white people." When fully outfitted, he began his campaign in earnest a few days later.

On the 16th I started on my journey to Lytton visiting the people along the [Thompson] river. After climbing mountains and valleys, and being careful in two or three places not to make a false step and fall into the river, I arrived at Lytton at about 6 p.m. After enquiring about a place to hold a meeting in for Sunday, I was told the trustee of the school lived three miles out of Lytton, and that he would be in about 9 o'clock in the morning. But I was told they never allowed anyone to hold meetings in it.

In the afternoon, I took the open-air, had about 40 Indians and a few white people to talk to. Had a very nice meeting. Sunday is the busiest day of the week. People come in for the week's provisions and then leave again towards night.

I sold six *War Cry*s, one man giving me a dollar for one. I started next morning for Lillooet up the Fraser, a distance of 42 miles, visiting the people along the river. It is a horse trail along the mountain sides, some places very steep and dangerous, but my faithful companion took me safely across. I stayed at the halfway house for the first night, arriving at Lillooet next day. Gold mining is the principal work here. Good-hearted people, very sociable and kind. Had a meeting in a barroom that night, and one in the open air on the night following; had good attention and they also helped in the singing. There are only seven white women there. Left a good impression and [had] an invitation to come again. I started for Clinton next, distance of 48 miles. Also visited the farms along the roads, and stayed that night on the top of Pavilion Mountain, about 5,000 feet above sea level. Arrived in Clinton the next day, I secured a hall for my meeting. Some told me that they had been wishing The Salvation Army would come to Clinton, but the people failed to come and hear The Salvation Army. Quite a few people were sick, and it being such a rough night may account for it. Some are longing for real salvation.

Captain Smith commenced a short second tour on September 24, 1890, from Spence's Bridge to Ashcroft where he arrived on October 3. At Lytton his meeting was in the Court House (where he sold twelve *War Crys*, but had no seekers), and in Lillooet he had to make do with the barroom of the hotel. At that town Captain Smith met Mr. Stevens, the Methodist minister, with whom he shared the Sunday services ("helping each other as best we could"), and during the week he conducted five salvation meetings which, all admitted, was something new for Lillooet.

Smith continues:

Got to Clinton on the 30th. Had two meetings here. Visited among the people. Got to Ashcroft on the 3rd of October. Had a prayer meeting with the young people here at 7 p.m. Real blessed time. Had a public meeting after. Very good meeting, but no souls. A man took up the collection here, and whether his chum was only putting in one bit or not I don't know but he told him he took nothing less than two bits (25¢). Held a meeting on Sunday morning, and as the Methodist minister was announced for night I went to another place 17 miles away, where they had only had a religious meeting once in four or five years. Had a real good meeting. Tears flowed freely, but none yielded. I am glad to say I am well in soul and body, and my horse is skukum (strong) [*The War Cry*, December 6, 1890].

In the late spring of 1891, Captain George Arkett and Cadet Jarvis joined the mountaineer team, this time travelling southeast from Kamloops into the ranching area of the Okanagan and keeping diary-like accounts of their adventures and experiences:

May 30, 1891: On Monday I go to Douglas Lake, but most of the men are away working on another ranch, so not many come to the meetings. We had a nice time. This morning I bid them goodbye and started for Stump Lake, some 25 miles. I only got a little way on the trail when I was lost. I turned here and there, over hills and into valleys. Soon it began to rain, and I could not see the sun, but after a few miles' ride I came to a large mountain and I rode my horse up to the top. Soon the sun came in sight and I made a fresh start for the open mountain country, and after going a few miles I saw two horses running in the distance. Then I started my horse faster. Soon I came to see the foot marks and I said, "Glory!" A few minutes brought me to the brow of a large hill. I looked into the distance. I could see a lake, and as I go on I see a straw stack. I said to myself, "This is nice." I began to take things quite easy then. Stopped on the side of a big mountain to feed my horses, also I asked God to bless the bread and meat the Chinaman gave me, and I did enjoy it.

Well, I have my dinner eaten, and I think my horse has had enough grass for a few hours' drive, so I shall put my pen and paper into the saddlebags and get on my horse and see where I am, for I am sitting on the ground on the side of a mountain writing and lost at the same time, but I shall try it again, so goodbye for this time.

Quite obviously, Captain Arkett did find his way out of those mountains and into others, for the next time we hear from him he has crossed the valley into the Cariboo area of British Columbia:

Monday was spent selling copies of *All the World* and visiting. I came to a little cabin by the side of the road and went to the door. The old man was eating dinner. He wanted me to tie my horse and come in to dinner. I had some venison and beans. The people call them cariboo strawberries. I also visited a woman, and she was so glad I had come to see her she cried for joy. It was something new. She said, "I am so glad you came to see me."

Tuesday, Captain Smith and myself stopped at a cabin by the side of the road. Out came a man, and he wanted to know if we had made any more saints. We told him God would make him a saint if he wanted to be one. He said, "No," and also stated that God did not live in this country. We asked him where God lived. He said, "God lives in Ireland." At this his frying pan caught fire on the stove and he tried to put it out, but could not. He muttered, "It burns like hell fire and purgatory." We told him our message and rode on.

Along the Fraser River the ride was sometimes precarious. Getting past rock slides was an especially dangerous task. One "nearly took my breath away," writes Captain Arkett. "So I let my horse go ahead and took hold of her tail and she pulled me up beautifully. At this place, if our horses had slipped, we would slide many hundred feet down the mountainside and into the river." Luckily, that did not happen and once past the danger, the twosome could relax "at a nice place where grass is growing, so our horses got a bite."

Arkett continues:

Bob and myself ate our lunch, and drank from a water-trough which leads the water from the mountainside to the Fraser River for mining. We sang that old chorus—

I'll be true, Lord, to Thee,
Whatever may befall
I shall surely conquer all

If I am but true to Thee.

And while we were many miles away from any Salvationists, God blessed us while we lifted our hearts to him in prayer. Hallelujah! [*The War Cry*, May 16, 1891].

Later in the year, Captain Arkett made a solo trip as far as Alkali Lake, from which, after a few hours' ride, he was again on the banks of the Fraser River.

Going up and down hill, winding around the mountains. I arrived at Dog Creek, which is a small place. I was received well, and made arrangements to have meetings here in future. Next day at it again, for I am a stranger in a strange land, and do not know how long it will take me to get out. I travelled through lots of timber country, and at a large hill I came across some men working on the road. In the valley below was an Indian town. The place is called Canoe Creek. I stopped with a farmer all night. Next day was Sunday, and it did seem strange to me, for I had been used to going to a "big go," and here I was, sitting by the side of the road talking to some men who were working on the road. I spent this night on some hay with a horse blanket over me. Of course it was better than some places I have seen.... Lillooet is the next place. I saw the miners washing and crushing rocks to secure the gold. They work hard after the gold that helps in this life, but they forget the pearl of greatest value. We had nice meetings, although no person came to Jesus.

Lytton was next. I could not find the key of the hall, so I had a meeting on the street, which had a good turn-out. Next day, after travelling some 14 miles, I came in sight of Old Man Mountain, near Spence's Bridge, so you see I was nearly home. Along the Thompson River could be seen Indians washing out gold and fishing. I sang a little song with the help of an old Indian, which was a treat to me, also prayed God to bless them. There are very few saved people in the mountains.... I have completed my 33 days' tour, travelling 633 miles. Also my horse and myself are strong, and victory is rising in the west [*The War Cry*, June 27, 1891].

Before the summer was over, Captain Arkett was off again on a second 200-mile tour, accompanied this time by Captain Robert Smith. The headline for his submission to *The War Cry* went like this: "Broke His Neck—Bit by a Rattlesnake—Horse-Flies and Prairie Chickens." The reader might have been a little disappointed, however, to find that the neck broken was that of the Captain Arkett's guitar which had been slung around Captain Smith's neck. "While trotting along," writes Smith, "my horse stumbled over a stone and my stirrup broke. I should have been all right, but my horse, as he was gaining his feet again, struck another, and this time landed me over his head, and as I had a guitar strapped to me, I fell on top of it, but hurt myself worse than the guitar, so both I and the guitar are in tune yet" [*The War Cry*, July 25, 1891].

It was also revealed that the rattlesnake bite had been inflicted on an Indian whom the mountaineers visited, not on one of them. But the hardships were real nonetheless. The trail to Williams Lake was "an old pack trail that used to be in use at one time to carry provisions to the Cariboo Mines" and was difficult to navigate for both horse and men. Having arrived at their northernmost destination, Soda Creek, and after holding a meeting in the street, Captains Arkett and Smith turned around to retrace their route to Kamloops. Apart from complaints concerning the thousands of "large flies" which bit both them and their horses, their comments are succinct and unrevealing. Of 150 Mile House they commented that "Drink is the great curse here." As for Clinton, it was "a place of deadness," but Ashcroft was beautiful, partly because it was "the only place we have testimonies and this is nice."

Further south, in the Nicola Valley, both weather and terrain were more accommodating. Arkett writes:

At Stump Lake I rested one day, also had lots of prairie chickens to eat. Chaperon Lake was the next place. This is a large cattle district, also large hay meadow. Sixteen men made themselves comfortable outside the cabin on a plank seat, and your humble servant preached the words of life.

They listened well. Minnie Lake is a little place, but the people were glad to see us come.

Coming across the mountains on Monday the cattle would run from me like deer. They are very wild. My last day, I traveled 38 miles. It was very warm, but we are happy. I came across a whiskey bottle and a little label on it, and these were the words, "Warranted to keep in any climate," and we have a Salvation that keeps us good, in any climate [*The War Cry*, September 5, 1891].

It must have been a source of much pleasure to many lonely people (mainly men) along the Fraser River to see and talk with itinerant preachers, even if they were bent on saving their souls. Many of them were lonely, and a few cut off from civilization. "I visited a poor old man," writes the cadet, "73 years of age, in a miserable state: so bad with rheumatics he could scarcely move one foot past the other; and although he has a good farm, and lots of stock on the mountains, yet he is living in a miserable hovel without the necessities of life. I determined I would stop with him overnight, and cut him some wood, and try and clean the place up a bit. I tried to point him to Jesus, read and prayed, and lay down to sleep on a pile of sacks in the corner, with my saddle for a pillow, and left the poor old fellow asleep."

In another lonely old shack, a man lived all alone, miles away from any human habitation. The Salvation Army outrider finally left him a *War Cry* and departed. The next time he visited he found the old man in great excitement, for he had read the Army's paper right through to the "Missing" columns, and there before him was his own name, and inquiries from friends who had lost sight of him for 35 years.

"After holding meetings in an old mining town, in the court-house," Jarvis continues, "about 30 present, nearly all the white people remaining in the place, I went on to a farmhouse. The people have been here 30 years, with a large family of young men, grown up, [who have] never been to a church or religious service of any kind, or seen a minister except Roman Catholic. Next at Big Bar (another old mining camp). Three families living here, white men married to Indian women, with large families of children. The men have at one time been Protestants, the wives and families have been baptized

Catholics, but there is now Christianity among them. Had a good meeting among them, in an old barroom, and tears were flowing down their cheeks."

"Down the [Fraser] river trail," writes Captain Arkett. "It is very rough. We visited two families in 46 miles. One man comes from England. He was educated for the ministry, and can play a violin to perfection. [His] woman does not know how to keep house, and there are eight or 10 children, mostly one size. You never saw any slum worse. We pleaded straight about their souls. We are going to do our best to get them straightened up and saved" [*All the World* (1892): 107].

And so the accounts went, with talk of Dog Creek and Alkali Lake, of mosquitoes and rattlesnakes, dangerous precipices and rapid rivers—and of many prayers, open-air meetings and testimonies. The Army's mountaineers rode into people's lives. They visited the small towns, and the farms and wayside ranches along the way, holding meetings wherever they happened to find themselves at night or could get a few people around during the day. Though they eventually rode into the sunset, they (and the Army they represented) were not soon forgotten.

Writing about the Army's mountaineer brigades in *All the World* in 1891, Florence Kinton offered this rather fanciful assessment of their achievement: "Artists came this way and sketched and painted to intoxication. Tourists travelled, and returned to tell their friends. Sportsmen and anglers hunted and fished in the lakes, till they could load the gun and bait the line no longer. Then a Salvationist chanced along, and he thought of the human beings, and wondered what about their spiritual necessities, and began to cast about to devise some plan by which this scattered population could be gathered in for Jesus, and taken hold of by the Army. After long thinking out and puzzling over, it was concluded that, since the mountain could not come to Mahomet, Mahomet should go to the mountain; or, more correctly, that the outriders should travel among the mountaineers."

Perhaps that was, in the Army way of describing things, an exaggeration of their achievement. But it nevertheless illustrated just how effectively the Army could adapt itself to local conditions. And, although the mountaineers may never have made many soldiers from their effort, they made the Army's presence felt far beyond the confines of the downtown barracks of Vancouver. The whole venture was, as one outrider put it, a "little bright light" for the many who never saw a clergyman from one year to the next.

FIVE

The Salvation Army's "Salvation Navy"

Evangelizing the Outports of Newfoundland and Along the Great Lakes' Shores

W E HAVE SEEN IT ALREADY. THE SALVATION ARMY
was quite adept at innovation—using every means
available to evangelize the nation. Of course, not
every scheme was successful, but they were tried
and, for a while at least, they not only boosted the Army's image but
reached a segment of the population which might not otherwise have
been reached. One notable enterprise of that kind was the Salvation
Navy. At the eastern end of Canada, in Newfoundland (not then part
of Confederation), schooners would fly the blood-and-fire flag along
the northern and southern coasts; and in central Canada they would
evangelize the many small towns along the shores of Lake Ontario.

The Sea-Girt Isle. That was how the early Canadian *War Cry*
nearly always described Newfoundland. And, though slightly romantic, it was an apt description. The ancient British colony, invaded by
The Salvation Army in 1886, was a patchwork of small fishing villages
(outports) scattered around a 10,000-mile coastline, whose indenta-
tions contained thousands of tiny coves, inlets and harbours, most of
them almost totally inaccessible by land and only precariously
approached by sea.

It was not long, therefore, before the Army's leaders realized that,
though they might easily secure a stronghold in the capital city of St.
John's and its few outlying towns, it would require something like a
naval detachment to bring the gospel message to the fisherfolk of
those otherwise-inaccessible outport communities. And this, in its
usual enterprising fashion, was what the Army did. They purchased,
or had built for them, two schooners; crewed them with sea-faring
Salvation Army officers, and, for a few years at least, sailed in and out
of the many harbours along the northeast and south coasts of Newfoundland, conducting Salvation Army meetings and inspiring many
of the locals to carry on the revival mission.

The idea for such a Salvation Navy sprang from the fertile mind of
the newly-appointed divisional commander, 24-year-old William
McIntyre who came to Newfoundland in November 1890. Why, he
reasoned, could the Army not have its own vessel, one that would
carry the gospel message to the remotest outports? Since catching the
local boats sometimes stranded him in an outport for weeks at a
time—a waste of valuable time for any revivalist—owning one's own

schooner, flying the Army blood-and-fire flag, would not only enhance the Army's image but considerably speed up the Army's plan to evangelize the far corners of the northern world. And so, in early 1891, McIntyre purchased a small schooner, renamed it the Glad Tidings, and with a crew of two (Captain James Bowering and Lieutenant William Bradbury), sent it on its maiden voyage to the coast of Labrador.

It was a wise beginning. For on that coast, every summer, thousands of Newfoundland fishermen took part in what was called the Labrador fishery. Many of them fished out of fixed locations, with a "room" on shore: they were called the stationers (or sometimes squatters or roomers). Others followed the fish, living aboard their schooners: they were the floaters (or green-fish catchers). While still a few others, perhaps tired of the annual trek, built themselves permanent shacks along the coast: they were the livyeres (a corruption of "live here"), always among the poorest of the poor. And nearly all of them were working for the planters, those entrepreneurs (pickpockets some fishermen called them) who advanced the necessary supplies in return for a large share of the fish which they then shipped to the markets.

Life on the Labrador in the 1890s—whether as a floater or stationer and especially for a livyere—was a precarious, physically exhausting affair. Those who lived on land, or who summered over to cure the fish, occupied tilts, mere hovels with only a barrel-stove and a bed. Their food, apart from fish, was of the most basic kind: salt beef and hard tack. "Fresh meat and vegetables are alike hard to procure," wrote Wilfred Grenfell. "No cow or horse exists. The domestic animal is represented only by the inevitable dog; the vegetable by the stringy cabbage or struggling turnip, whose leaves alone attain to economic value.... These people neither need nor expect luxuries: sugar and milk are very rarely used—tinned milk being too expensive, molasses being cheaper than sugar, and also margarine than butter" [*Vikings of Today* (1895)].

Those who laboured aboard the vessels (with occasional shore visits), fared a little better, but they were crowded and at the mercy of the master. They received no wages, and saw no money, but traded their share of the fish for supplies and food. "When seven men fish one trap," writes Grenfell, "the total catch is divided into 14 shares—seven for the planter and seven for the men.... Or when a man fishes his own net with four men I saw the value divided into twelve shares—four for the master, four for the trap, and one each for the men, so that every man gets every twelfth fish." If the fishing was good, and in the 1890s it was not, the fishermen could at least survive and perhaps sell their fish for a few dollars; if it was not, they merely engaged in the fishery as a means of subsistence. It was a hard life, to be sure, but one to which Newfoundlanders had become accustomed—poverty, physical hardship and danger were sure facts of their daily life, all of which they stoically accepted.

It was to these men (and a lot of women as well) that The Salvation Army hoped to bring the gospel message, providing religious companionship for those who had already become Salvationists and perhaps converting others to the cause. In June and July of 1891, stocked with essential food supplies as well as fishing gear and salt to cure the fish (for they intended to pay their way), the Glad Tidings cruised the Labrador coast, its officers not only preaching at the various shore stations, catching a few fish in the meantime, but also, as the only religious presence among the fishermen (save for the occasional appearance of the missionary, Wilfred Grenfell), making some converts for the Army. Some of whom, it is known, when they returned to their hometowns in the fall, continued the expansion of the Army by holding revival meetings on their own until officers could be appointed

After wintering over in Newfoundland's Bay Roberts, in the summer of 1892, the Glad Tidings, this time crewed by three Salvation Army officers (Captain James Bowering, Lieutenants William Parsons and Frederick Day), again cruised the Labrador coast, having had "a very successful run of work" among the fishermen. Before they set out, the officer-crew had gathered a list of all Army soldiers who would be going to the Labrador, with the names of the schooners they had sailed in. "Then sometimes," writes Florence Kinton in *All the World*, "when they cruise around, as they come in sight of a fishing boat, they hail her, and with flag signals find out her name, and if on reference to their list they see any of our men are aboard, they go to visit them, talk and pray with them, ask how their souls are prospering, deal with them personally, help them in any difficulties, and do all in their power to comfort and cheer any who may be failing. Wherever the boat may go, she is known by her colours and courteously welcomed with kindly greeting and inquiries as to her provisions, etc., and if she should be in need of anything, the lack is liberally supplied."

When the fish were plentiful, the crew of the Glad Tidings would also cast a line to add to the supply of fish given them by grateful fishermen, to help pay for expenses. Kinton continues:

> Some boats will give them the cod raw and some made. The former is about half the value of the latter, for after it is caught it has to be prepared, split so that the cod liver may be carefully preserved for oil, cleaned, and thrown into the salt barrel, afterwards to be spread out on frames, or fish flakes, made of spruce boughs, arranged so that the sunshine and the air can get through and thoroughly dry them then spread out and piled up, to be exchanged for cheques with the merchants' agents along the coast.
>
> Often the weather is rough, the schooners cannot venture out to sea; then the sailors have nothing to do but put in the time washing the decks and curing their fish. These are the days when, far from home and wife and child, any human face and any diversion is welcomed, whatever there may have been of prejudice before, to break the lonesome, monotonous hours. Then our officers hold their salvation meetings among them, until fair weather breaks out again and their nets may be spread once more, telling them of the man Christ Jesus, who still is near in the night watches, as they drift about, as he once was, long ago, when other fishermen saw him come walking across the waters full in their view, calming their troubled hearts with quiet words, "It is I; be not afraid."

When the Glad Tidings returned to St. John's at the end of the 1892 fishing season, her crew, who had brought back a "few quintals" of fish with them, conducted four days of special meetings during which they regaled their vast audiences with their seafaring adventures and soul-saving experiences.

The following summer, 1893, brought a new challenge for the Army's Salvation Navy. Renovated and refitted, and with a new crew made up of Captain Robert Bowering and Lieutenants Cooper and Bishop, the small schooner was sent on a scouting expedition to the south coast of Newfoundland, to determine which outports (not already invaded) might be worth invading. Not very many were, of course: most of them were simply too small, and many were Roman Catholic, Protestants being a minority along that coast. But even in those that didn't adopt the Army—in places like Belleoram, Harbour Breton, La Plant and Pool's Cove—the schooner's crew, along with the district officer, Henry Freeman, gave the religious-starved inhabitants a taste of salvation glory. In some small outports, such as Seal Cove, where there had been no religious presence for many years, the fishermen were waiting for someone to provide them with a permanent ministry, and as the crew of the Glad Tidings were the first to evangelize their community, they adopted The Salvation Army as their religious denomination.

Though much good work was done along those shores, and on the Labrador coast, it soon became clear that the Glad Tidings was simply too small to withstand the rough seas of the Newfoundland coast. If the work was to be continued, a larger vessel would be needed. In 1893, therefore, Adjutant John Read, the new divisional commander, decided to have a larger schooner built, naming it the Salvationist. She would, *The War Cry* announced, be built during the winter of 1893 by Mr. Frank Warr at Robert's Arm—a 36-ton yacht-rigged schooner, 58 feet long, with a breadth of 17 feet, at a cost of $1,700:

> The Salvationist will carry a complete set of Salvation Army accoutrements. She is fitted, at a push, to sleep 25 persons. She can be converted, with little trouble, into a floating barracks, capable of seating 150 people. She will carry, in addition to the essentials of a full-rigged vessel, a tent for shore meetings, a number of folding chairs, a supply of medicines, a circulating library, hymn books, Bibles, *War Crys*, as well as all the machinery of an ordinary corps. Her officers and crew will likely number three or four, and their

plan of procedure is as follows: The Salvationist will leave the island with the fishing fleet, accompanying them to the Labrador coast. She will then commence cruising. From harbour to harbour, where little groups of fishermen locate for the purpose of curing their fish, she will carry the gospel. Dropping anchor in the bays, she will dispatch one or more of her crew to shore. Sometimes the tent will be brought into use. At others, the fishermen will be invited to come on board the schooner, where a meeting will be held. In addition to this, the officers will keep in touch with the large number of our soldiers who work all summer on the coast. Thousands of men work up in that lonely region for months, and it can readily be understood that the presence of bright, happy, singing Salvationists will be appreciated and make a blessing. God speed the Salvationist.... Her hull will be painted black. Her fittings, boat and houses, white, and she will carry a tri-colour band of the Army red, yellow and blue, round her gunwale [*The War Cry*, May 19, 1894].

For a few years, then, The Salvation Army's flag flew from the mainmasts of two schooners, the Glad Tidings and the Salvationist. The latter, after she had been commissioned in typical Salvation Army fashion on July 25, 1894, set sail from Newfoundland with her rejuvenated sister for Labrador. At Twillingate, after some campaigning by their officers (and their new divisional commander, Frank Morris), the two schooners went their separate ways. The Salvationist—with her crew of Captain Parsons, master; Lieutenant Cooper, mate; Lieutenant Moulton, second mate; Cadet Green, deck hand; and Cadet Downey, cook; and Majors Robert and Susie Tilley as guests—proceeded to the Labrador coast to continue the Army's annual mission to the seasonal fishermen, while the Glad Tidings—with her crew of Captain Gosling, Cadet Hiscock, Cadet Burry and Major and Mrs. Richard Morris as special guests—undertook a tour of Notre Dame Bay settlements.

For Major Morris, a green hand from Canada, this was both his first experience along the coast and his introduction to the New-foundland style of Army worship. And it was, what with seasickness on the way to Bonavista, his first meal of cod tongues ["topped any-thing I have eaten since coming to Newfoundland"] and a good taste of ranting revivalism, a memorable one. But finally they reached Notre Dame Bay where their tour would really begin, and here is how Major Morris described it:

At 1:30 a.m. we hoisted sail and weighed anchor, the sea lovely. Captain Parsons promised to land me clear of seasickness at Twillingate, which he did on Sunday afternoon, just when the march was on the streets. We had been becalmed, and had to lay to for some 12 hours, thus detaining us.

At night we all made for the barracks, which was crowded, and had a most beautiful time. At midnight we closed the meeting, without souls; they sat all over the place full of conviction, but no break.

On Monday a few more repairs and fittings were done by the crew of The Salvationist, the Glad Tidings arrived bringing good news. They had landed on an island, and had what people call "prayers," which had not been in that place for years, and three souls were saved. All the people left in a state of revival. Captain Gosling had some difficulty in getting his crew on board. It seemed to become a test to desert the schooner and go and live with these people, so glad were they to hear of Jesus' love. The crew declare they never attended or led such a meeting before.

At night we marched in full force, both crews united, and at it we went till 11 p.m., first meeting, then up we went for a pull, and were rewarded after hard fighting. Conviction was rampant, and everywhere they seemed spellbound and struck. Just one yielded, and for three quarters of an hour she shouted, screamed and tore round, tears flowed, and she beat the seat and struggled. At last, at last! Oh, my, a yell and a jump! If she had had as many devils as Mary Magdalene she could not have seemed more beset. All the officers and soldiers danced and shouted, and for an hour a real Salvation jubilation went on.

After the Salvationist had sailed for Labrador, the Glad Tidings with the Morrises, continued their evangelical tour of Notre Dame Bay. In many communities, they found their people in near poverty. The men had caught little fish, and there was no prospect of food for the winter. "Some of the Green Bay fishermen," wrote one reporter, "have not known the like for 40 years." Many Salvationists had no money at all, not enough to purchase a *War Cry* which, stated Morris, they just loved to read. "Oh, how I wish I could give them to them. Shut in so, away from the world, anxious to hear all the Salvation Army news and cannot get it! One *Cry* will be passed from one to the other, and read, and then sent away." And yet he found the people happy, and always ready for a grand hallelujah meeting.

A little after seven o'clock they began to assemble, some of them carrying chairs to fill up the spare room, not having a seat, and taking them home again after the meeting. One old man hung on until his poor old face beamed with joy and tears rolled down his cheeks, and voice and strength were gone shouting and clapping his hands. Our first meeting lasted until 11 o'clock, then we went in for a real good prayer meeting. Not a soul moved until the next meeting was over. At something after one o'clock in the morning we began to cool down a little. At last a break came. One sister came, then another. After some earnest pleading and tears one jumped up, and it seemed to me that she wanted to fly; she bounded around and no mistake. Everybody was dancing, jumping, singing, roaring, drumming happy. Oh, my! Lift up the scenes and look, the whole pot boiling. I cannot describe the scene! You must imagine religion in the extreme extravagance, and then you have one-fifth part of it. The like my eyes never saw before. The people said, "If only you stay another night, what a time we would have." It seemed to me a providence God had ordered for me to depart, or I would surely kill myself to save these people (*The War Cry,* September 8, 1894).

Meanwhile, aboard the Salvationist, Ensign Abraham Tilley, second-in-charge of Newfoundland (and a seasoned Newfoundlander), had proceeded to the Labrador coast. In 1894, the fishery along that coast was a complete failure, and whatever little money the fishermen had saved was wiped out in one of the worst financial disasters in Newfoundland's history. Theirs was, quite literally, a struggle for survival—one which even The Salvation Army could do little to alleviate. But, along with the visits of the noted medical missionary, Wilfred Grenfell, those of the Salvationist were much appreciated. To the few—and often suffering—inhabitants and summer residents of Double Island, Hopedale, Turnavik and Indian Harbour the regular appearance of the Army's schooner, with her crew of dedicated missionaries, ready to ferry the sick to the Grenfell Hospital or hold a hallelujah meeting or even conduct a funeral, was a welcome sight indeed. And to Salvationists pining for the company of like-minded religionists, a visit from the Salvationist was like a gift sent from heaven. As one comrade at Square Islands put it, "Well, comrades, I could not sleep this past night I felt so anxious to get to knee-drill." For a few years, at least, the loneliness and religious privation of the Labrador fishermen and women were occasionally (and very gratefully) alleviated by the presence of the good ship Salvationist.

Somewhat later, after General Booth had made his visit to Newfoundland (September 18-19, 1894), the adventurous Major Morris decided to visit Salvationists on the south coast, the Glad Tidings being then touring that coast and awaiting him at Fortune. She was, said Morris, "to be our home and support to cross Fortune Bay." But the weather, as so often happened, dictated otherwise. After 27 hours beating against a strong wind, with everyone seasick and drenched to the skin, they made just 18 miles to Grand Bank, instead of the 20 miles to Seal Cove. "We were," wrote Morris, "only five miles nearer our desired appointment for 27 hours' work and all our danger and seasickness."

Such were the happenstances of Newfoundland travel by schooners propelled by sails. A wild ocean at one moment, a calm one a moment later. For within the hour, Morris continues, the wind had changed fair, and within three hours they were at their destination, Seal Cove:

The fishermen saw us, and six of them put off in a dory to

meet us, and jumped on board. Uncle seized the tiller, and every man took his post, and just like trained and skilful pilots did they run us right into that dangerous harbour.... The exciting run in, the commotion ashore, the glad faces, and welcomes, and running of children, as I stepped on shore, in my oilcoat and cap, to grasp the hard, brawny hands of the toilers of the deep, and to share their joy, why I almost wished to stay with them....

This place was once a deathtrap. Boats, loaded with spiritous liquors from the island of St. Pierre, which is only a few miles away, under French government, used to come in. The purchase of their product—fish, etc.—sometimes a whole summer's fishing would go this way by many of the inhabitants. Those spirits used to produce 10 times the amount of much more evil spirits among them. But, oh, what a change! No more smugglers, no more drinking, and nearly in every home you can find the family altar and some members of the family having a practical knowledge of God and salvation, and many homes have every member converted.

All in all, the Army's Salvation Navy was an exciting and worthwhile enterprise—quite in keeping with its intention to evangelize by whatever means seemed appropriate. And, in Newfoundland, a navy was entirely appropriate. Unfortunately, and to the great disappointment of many Newfoundlanders, by 1898, the costs were simply too great to continue such a service. The fishermen themselves, in those lean years of the 1890s, when even some of Newfoundland's mercantile enterprises failed, were not able to support the upkeep of two schooners. In 1898, therefore, the Glad Tidings and the Salvationist sailed for the last time as Salvation Army schooners and in 1900, both vessels were sold. But they had, without any doubt, changed the lives of many people along those remote stretches of Newfoundland coast.

When Commandant Herbert Booth, commander of the Canadian Territory (1892-1896), called on Canadian Salvationists in 1894 to celebrate his father's jubilee year (the 50th anniversary of his dedication to his Christian calling) he did so announcing 50 jubilee schemes intended to boost soldierly morale and address recent declines in the Army's ranks. Among them was an addition to the Salvation Navy. Proposing to buy a small steamship to sail the Great Lakes and evangelize towns along its shores, Herbert rationalized the plan as follows:

> We have internal as well as external seas in Canada. Within our immense area we can boast of lakes larger than whole countries of Europe. By means of rivers and canals, which link up those stupendous fresh water seas, we can traverse thousands of miles, and reach almost hundreds of ports.
>
> Now, why not avail ourselves of these waterways for carrying the message of salvation precisely as they are utilized in the interests of commerce. Everybody knows it is cheaper to travel by water than by land, especially when it becomes a question of carrying numbers. We have thought the matter out with great care, and have decided to purchase a steam yacht of our own. The circumstances leading to the decision are interesting. Last year when travelling with the Praying Gang, the New Canadians and the Flying Squadron, I became convinced of what might be done and what help rendered our poorest corps by means of more such gangs. Every time, however, I made any definite proposition, I was confronted by the tremendous obstacle of railway travelling. The distances are so great, the expenses so heavy, that it is sheer bankruptcy to attempt anything by means of the iron horse. What we wanted was a kind of travelling house, in which a brigade could sleep and live, when unable to cover cheaply a whole distance between one town and another where we have corps. Something that would make them independent of billets when they were impossible of finding, and yet some way by which our companies could travel from place to place at a minimum of cost. I sent to see what the cost of chartering would be. It was stupendous; we could almost buy a boat right off for very little more. Then we looked around. We found steamboats of the kind we required, to be had at a very low charge, and we decided to purchase....

How shall we use her? In all sorts of ways. Immediately the sunshine clears the surface of the lake we shall have her underway. The coast towns and those adjacent thereto will be fortunate. She will visit them as fast as she can get around. One trip she will take a training garrison of lads or lasses who, while being trained on board, will attack the towns en route. Another trip she will carry a first-class singing brigade. Another trip she will take down a group of Ontario officers to the east, and bring back an exchange gang of eastern officers to Ontario. Both gangs setting the country on fire as they come and go. Another trip it may be possible for her to push through to Lake Erie, and up through Lake Superior to the Lake of the Woods, where she could take on a party of candidates from the northwest, and convey them east at half the cost of present railway transit.... As soon as we can secure her she will be dedicated and christened the SS William Booth in honour of the General's jubilee. Her first trip will be taken this summer with Mrs. Booth and a party of female cadets aboard [The War Cry, May 9, 1894].

It was a bold and ambitious plan, one very much in keeping with the Army's intention to evangelize every corner of the nation. But, though exciting for a while, it was a venture fraught with mishaps and unforeseen expenses, and never did fulfil Herbert Booth's expectations.

But, back to the purchase itself. The 54-ton boat, 72 feet long with a 12 foot beam, and with a 20 horsepower motor, was purchased from a Mr. Macdonald of Hamilton, Ont., who had it built to his specifications. "It could not," commented Herbert Booth, "have been more conveniently arranged for our needs." She was dedicated and christened the SS William Booth on July 31, 1894. With an obvious sense of humour, someone (perhaps even the commandant himself) had included the popular Army song, We Are Out On the Ocean Sailing, but it might, suggested a reporter, be too early to sing the chorus, "All the storms will soon be over" before "she has faced even one." But it was a buoyant ceremony, full of salty witticisms, and when it was asked how many the boat could accommodate, and the answer given, "One hundred and thirty at a pinch," the commandant remarked (to full laughter) that he would hate to be the 130th "at a pinch." And then the newly-painted SS William Booth took as many as she could on a cruise around Toronto harbour "into the shadows of the evening, leaving a long trail of quivering silver behind in her wake."

It was an auspicious beginning, and continued so for several days. Just after the dedication ceremony, the vessel with a crew of eight, Staff-Captain Jewer in command, and with Commandant Booth aboard, left the Yonge Street wharf for Hamilton, Ont., and other towns westward into Lake Erie as far as Detroit. At St. Catharines, Ont., the reception, deemed to be typical of what lay ahead, was described by the local newspaper, *The Journal:*

> About 6:30 p.m., on Thursday, there arrived at lock eight here, a handsome little steamer flying the colours of The Salvation Army, and in charge of a number of members of that body dressed in man-o'-war costume.
>
> The boat is named the William Booth, and will be used to convey auxiliary members to various points on the lake where regular posts of the Army are not located. Besides the officers and crew, there was on board Commandant Booth, a son of the Founder of the Salvationists. They were met at the wharf by a large turnout of the members here, and many citizens, and were received with cheers and prayer, as well as music by their band, which was supplemented by several good players on the steamer. After cordial shaking of hands, Mr. Booth and the officers in charge of the city corps entered a carriage, and in the meantime the jolly boat of the vessel was hoisted on a lorry. Four sailors, handling oars, took seats in the boat and the procession marched up Ontario and King Streets to the courthouse where a brief halt was made and Commandant Booth was introduced to the crowd by the captain, who asked all present to fire a volley of welcome to him, which was done by a hearty cheer. Mr. Booth heartily thanked all present for their welcome. He speaks with a strong, clear English accent, which there is no misunderstanding, and in the space of a few minutes gave a

concise history of the Army and all its work, and closed with an appeal to look well to their soul's keeping and their walk through life, and in fact, during that short time, preached a better practical sermon than many a clergyman could do in a week.

The procession then proceeded to their barracks, Geneva Street, which was crowded with people, and the remainder of the evening spent in listening to addresses from Mr. Booth, and also relations from those who accompanied him on the yacht of their former lives, conversion and experiences as Salvationists, the intervals being filled up with good singing and music.

Whatever may be the opinions of some people regarding the merits of the Army, certain it is that they are eminently sincere and practical in their work. We wish them and their new venture in preaching the truth along the shores of our lakes and rivers a hearty Godspeed.

The next ports of call were Welland, Ont., and Buffalo, N.Y. (for a four-day campaign), and then to Port Colborne, Ont. One of the Tars (as they called themselves) then picks up the story:

We shoved off from Buffalo for Port Colborne, leaving there Thursday morning for Selkirk. Everything was beautiful and the boys were all in good spirits, and within two miles of Selkirk, just as the band was going to strike up to practise, to our surprise we came to a sudden stop, and we soon discovered that we were on the rocks, then every effort was put forth to get her off, but all without success. It was about 10 in the morning when we struck the rocks, and it was now seven, and we were announced to be in Selkirk that night, and as we didn't want to disappoint the people we lowered the lifeboat, and as many as could rowed to shore, a distance of over two miles, and then walked three miles to the town, and after partaking of a hearty supper we hurried off to the meeting. The fact that we had been wrecked caused a great sensation. The people came from all directions, and by the time we reached the Baptist church it was impossible to find seating room.

Next morning we hurried off to see what had become of the ship and the rest of the crew, and we just got there in time to see her being towed back to Port Colborne by the tug Golden City to be repaired.

As her crew set off for Port Colborne to rejoin their vessel, bad news met them. Their ship, in dry dock, had caught fire. "The boys were to commence painting at daylight, and while the oil was heating, by some reason it ignited." The fire, in a place where no water was available, was devastating; the hull was saved, and the engine and boiler were not seriously damaged, but nearly the whole interior was gutted. The cost of repair was $2,000; exactly the amount paid for the vessel in the first place.

But repaired she was. Herbert Booth was determined (call it vanity or devotion) that the SS William Booth would be at Brockville, Ont., when his father, the General, arrived there in October on the eastern leg of his second visit to Canada. He would, it was decided, travel through the Thousand Islands to Kingston, Ont., and then as far as Port Hope, Ont., where, after a day at Peterborough, Ont., he would return to Montreal and cross to the United States to continue his tour there.

But, again, the mishaps outlived the pleasures in people's memories. It started well enough. "The waters tried to engulf her," wrote the English *War Cry* correspondent, "the flames to cremate her, yet here she was [at Brockville], buoyant as a cork, her myriad pinioned rigging smiling and bowing, and all anxiety to welcome to her bosom her great namesake and General. As she lay alongside Brockville dock, she looked the very embodiment of a gladsome Salvationist spirit.... The weather put on its sweetest aspect, and in a few minutes we were joyously navigating the sinuosities of the Thousand Islands. These beauty spots vary from hundreds of acres to mere land specks, surmounted, perhaps, by a single tree. Upon many of them thousands of dollars have been lavished—chiefly by rich Americans—in the erection of summer residences, hotels, etc., while many are the favourite camping grounds of religious bodies. To these the stirring strains of salvation music wafted from the Naval Brigade's Band, and wave-of-fering thank-yous would be sent back by the dwellers in these paradisical abodes" [*The War Cry*, November 10, 1894].

Just outside Gananoque, Ont., however, her engines became silent. Making much faster time than expected, it was decided to idle for a while and enjoy the scenery. But when the engines were primed, they failed to start. A broken pipe prevented her from getting up steam and everyone aboard had to wait until, as one person put it, "a tug came and ignominiously dragged us in." The only benefit was that William Booth had a new story to tell and new lessons to be learned from the experience, telling his Gananoque audience, to "never stop because you are going too fast, for, if you do, the devil may keep you from starting again. I watched our steamer going up the St. Lawrence, and it needed some sort of skill to tell which way we were going. You had to fix your eye upon some landmark. Then the fire was let out; she stopped, and began to go back. So with a great many people—they begin red-hot. They say, 'Let us wake everybody up.' Then almost imperceptibly they cool down, down, down, til presently the fire goes out, and they begin to drift back down the stream."

No doubt, to later audiences, the General would have yet other stories to tell, based on a further mishap as the vessel grounded on a sandbank near Picton, Ont., and all the efforts of her crew were futile to set her free. "The General," writes Arnold Brown, "made aware of the mishap, came on deck, and, seeing the confusion, took control, ordering the entire ship's company to one side of the vessel. At a given signal, he said, they were to run to the other gunwale, and at another signal, back again. By this means the boat was rocked off the sandbar and into safer waters. So did the Founder demonstrate his ability not only to be General of a great Army, but also qualified commodore of the Canadian Salvation Navy!" [*What Hath God Wrought*, p. 100].

The remainder of the trip to Belleville, Ont., went without incident and, even though there had been minor mishaps previously, the whole adventure by water was considered worth the effort. What William Booth actually thought of the venture is not known, but it seems that his son, Herbert, was quite confident that this part of his Salvation Navy would reap great rewards in terms of revivals and souls won.

In the summer of 1895, therefore, the SS William Booth plied the waters of both Lake Erie and Lake Ontario, with a crew of 19 men, most of whom, except the engineer and skipper, were musicians and evangelists, led by Commodore Adjutant McGillivray. She left Toronto on May 15 for the western half of her mission trip, the *Globe* suggesting that "citizens who can manage it should certainly avail themselves of the opportunity of seeing the yacht sail out of the harbour. It will be an interesting sight."

And it was to be also an interesting trip. Mainly because American law, it was suddenly discovered, prevented a Canadian vessel from coasting along its shores and sailing from one American port to the next. Instead it would be necessary for the William Booth to call at a Canadian port, exit customs, and sail to an American port, then sail back to another Canadian port, again exit customs, and sail to the next American port, and so on. It meant that the vessel spent much of her time crisscrossing Lake Erie from one port on the Canadian side to another on the American. Thus, Sarnia, Ont., to Detroit, back to Windsor, Ont., then to Monroe, Mich., back to Leamington, Ont., then to Sandusky, Ohio, and so the trip continued. It was, stated one of the crew, an exhausting way of travelling, crossing the lake in all kinds of weather just to meet the deadlines, but in their *War Cry* reports they were as up-beat as ever.

> Monday morning finds us pulling out from Windsor [, Ont.,] for Monroe, [Mich.,] a place that neither fears God nor man. We trust their hearts may be touched by the pleading influence of the lassies. The sail across the lake was the best of the season, for with a good stiff breeze our little boat wafted along, and all with merry hearts and smiling faces, enjoyed the rolling of the boat. We reached Amherstburg, [Ont.,] and here we were received with open arms. We spent three days in Amherstburg, and profitable ones they were, marching and playing, and practising. We left for Toledo, [Ohio], early on Friday morning and arrived there shortly after dinner. The people were expecting us and we were received with some amount of display. God bless Toledo. We marched through the city on arriving, and formed up at the barracks at 7 p.m. Our first appointment was in a large

Methodist church. We held a good open-air and then proceeded to the church where a goodly number were awaiting. We had a good, lively, salvation meeting. Our dear adjutant read and, as usual, invited sinners to the cross, and we believe that good will follow our first attempt in Toledo. We will be here till Tuesday morning. Everybody pray for the brigade.

Arriving back in Toronto on August 9, the Naval Brigade, with just two days' rest, set sail again for the east, with stops at Port Hope and Cobourg, Ont., and 15 other towns along Lake Ontario, with a final stop at Ogdensburg, N.Y., on September 7 and 8. It was, from all accounts, just the kind of evangelistic outreach Herbert Booth had intended.

In June 1896, however, Herbert Booth received his farewell orders with a new appointment as commander of the forces in Australia. Taking his place was his sister, Evangeline, and when she arrived on June 11 for her grand welcome, she entered Toronto aboard the SS William Booth having been ferried across from Buffalo. And when, a few weeks later, she went to Hamilton, Ont., for another welcome, though she travelled by train, the headquarters staff and band were transported there and back by the SS William Booth. And so it seemed that the accident-prone vessel would continue her Great Lakes mission. But, for some now-unknown reason, that is the last we hear of the stout little vessel.

Perhaps the realization had struck home that the costs were outweighing the benefits, for on several occasions *The War Cry* had made special pleas for the maintenance and repair of the vessel. Or, more likely, such a mission was not a priority with Evangeline Booth: she was a land person, advocating the much cheaper bicycle as a means of travel, and was soon devoting her energies to promoting the children's work (the Children's Village and fresh air camps) and the Social Farm (where she took pleasure in riding horses). Whatever the reason, after July of 1896, we hear nothing more of the SS William Booth. One presumes she was sold, but, like all terminated ventures of the Army, the end, unlike the beginning, receives no notice. We take pleasure in the fact that, for a brief time at least, the Salvation

Navy as a branch of The Salvation Army was able to evangelize in a manner that was both different and, one assumes, quite effective.

SIX

Evangeline Booth's Imaginative Approach to Evangelism

I T IS THE EVENING OF NOVEMBER 21, 1897. TONIGHT COMmander Evangeline Booth will deliver her "Miss Booth in Rags" performance at Toronto's Massey Hall. Blanche Read, one of her officers, arrives at 6:30 for the 7:30 event, sees hundreds of people waiting to get in, but finds that the doors are locked against them. "What a pity," she murmurs, as she approaches the doorkeeper. "Lucky for you," he assures her, as he looks at her reserved-seat ticket. "We have had to close the doors, because the hall is quite filled. All these people here just cannot be accommodated. Miss Booth, it seems, is the greatest attraction we have seen since Massey Hall has been opened. Who is she, anyway?"

She is, of course, the well-known daughter of William Booth and, at this moment, is commander of the Salvation Army forces in Canada. She was born Evelyne Cory Booth—has since legally changed her name to Evangeline—on Christmas Day 1865, a few months after her father had begun his mission to the people of East London. And so she grew up along with The Christian Mission and, while still a teen, saw it transformed into The Salvation Army. She was, therefore, a Salvationist to the core—had professed conversion, worn the uniform and begun her career as an officer by selling *War Cry*s.

"She claims," wrote her biographer, "that she became the champion seller of *War Cry*s in the Army, and her position was on the pavement outside Liverpool Street Station close to a big public house. She reduced her business to a system. First, she read the current issue of the paper with careful intent. Then, she made a list of all the countries and towns mentioned in its columns. This list she committed to memory, and she would then pursue passers-by, telling them that there was an interesting piece in *The War Cry* about this or that place. Over and over again it meant a sale" (P.W. Wilson, *Evangeline Booth*, p. 59).

From that auspicious beginning she graduated to preaching and, then, with native ingenuity and imaginative daring, she disguised herself as a London flower-seller, just to reach and share her testimony with the ragged girls who plied their trade at the base of the Piccadilly Circus fountain. Though probably not as rash as Railton or Dowdle, nor as flamboyant as Lawley, Evangeline Booth nevertheless embraced the Army's spirit of aggressiveness—of innovativeness, daring and individual initiative.

And she continued to do so when, in 1896, she became the field commissioner of The Salvation Army in Canada. A brilliant speaker, a gifted actress and an accomplished musician, she had also a flair for creative evangelism.

One of the most talked-about events of her Canadian tenure (1896-1904) was her Miss Booth in Rags performances. They were among the memorable events of many Ontario cities and towns. At Massey Hall in Toronto, in the City Hall in Montreal, at barracks and town halls across Canada, she brought her audiences to tears as she re-created her early experiences among London's poor. As she would do, so many times later throughout the United States, when as The Commander in Rags or in The Tale of a Broken Heart she re-assumed the character of a Cockney flower-seller and, dressed appropriately, regaled her audience with tales of broken and mended hearts.

The Toronto *Globe* stated that Miss Booth's performance drew to Massey Hall "the most enormous crowd that has ever surged around its doors ... the manager of the hall estimates that not less than 10,000 people tried to secure admission. The Governor-General and Lady Aberdeen, Lady Marjory Gordon and party from Government House were among those present, occupying a box near the platform."

> She [Miss Booth] was dressed in a grey and rather frayed woolen dress, the sleeves of which came just below the elbow, and had a white apron and a plain shawl above it, the shawl being worn in the East London fashion, that is, pinned around the neck and falling down below the waist. Her hair was dressed in Whitechapel style, and her shoes, decidedly worn, were tied with strings....
>
> It was she explained, the beginning of self-denial week in the Canadian department of the Army, and she desired to speak of the beacon lights set for those who would follow Jesus. She built upon the platform during her address a cross, the various parts of which had upon them the words obedience, sympathy, sacrifice, love and crowning. As Miss Booth paused in her remarks, and each block was added to the model, a choir stationed out of sight in one of the

corridors sang a verse of a hymn appropriate to the word on the block.

In a voice that "sweetly resonated" through the hall, Evangeline Booth told stories of how, as a young girl, she had disguised herself as a London Cockney, and visited the courts. "When cases were tried and the prisoner convicted and she heard the wail of the wife, or the cry of the daughter, or the old man's sob of 'My son, my son,' she went to the sorrowing ones and offered to visit their friends in jail and take messages for them.... After delivering the message she spent the time going from cell to cell and corridor to corridor praying and talking. At last the officials learned who the ragged little girl was, and when they let her out they would whisper, 'Get another case and come again.' They told her later how when she was praying the prisoners in the upper corridors would put their ears to the grating to catch the words" [*The War Cry*, November 22, 1897].

At other times, quite often in fact, Evangeline Booth would re-create her experiences as a London flower-seller—the occasions in her youth when she had assumed that role in order to reach the lower classes. She was, writes her biographer, "conscious of the line drawn between herself and the people at the base of society that she wished to win. She must cross that line and feel within herself what it is to earn a living on the pavement. Bernard Shaw's *Pygmalion* was a flower girl who was turned into a lady. Evangeline Booth decided to be a lady turned into a flower girl. She clothed herself in a ragged costume and took her place on the steps of the fountain at Piccadilly Circus."

The other flower girls in their shawls did not know what to make of her. Her hands were smooth. Her voice was gentle. But her boots were worn, her stockings were darned, her dress was tattered and her demeanour was wistful. They pitied the "dearie" who came down in the world so low as this. Not that she was slow at the game. She sold as many flowers as the best of them [Wilson, p. 64]. And soon she had won her own small congregation of street people to whom she ministered in her own inimitable way.

It was this period of her life that she presented to her Canadian and (later) American audiences. Always careful to advertise her performances as representations and not mere acting (because Canadians were wary of mixing drama and religion), she drew thousands of people to the Army who might otherwise have ignored it. As one *War Cry* report stated: "The audience applauded and wept, laughed and cried as they beheld that child of God in tatters before them, as delicate almost as the flowers she carried in the basket on her arm; and this was not a performance, it was a representation of real life—of a life lived by one who was portraying it."

With a superb sense of the dramatic, Evangeline Booth would choreograph her performance so that while she spoke, the soft sweet sound of a children's choir (all dressed in white) literally floated above her. On other occasions she was preceded onto the platform by a group of officers dressed in various costumes whom she would use in her performance, and then she appeared (to thunderous applause), a seemingly "lonely figure clad in a ragged skirt and torn apron, a gaudily-coloured shawl around her shoulders." At an appropriate moment, she might draw a small child to her bosom, explaining that she was one of the orphans who were now under the Army's care and who would lead the expected procession of people who would place gifts on the altar. Other times, when she described how music alone had the power to break down the barriers in the slums, she would pick up her accordion and play *Home, Sweet Home*. And sometimes, to enhance the moment, she would often use her own adopted children, Pearl and "Little" Willie (who sang beautiful duets), along with live animals, to lend reality to her message. Here is how *The War Cry* described one such event:

> Miss Booth in vivid language, pictured to us first her little home in the slums, with its bare floor and few pieces of simple furniture. In her lecture she took us down into the miserable cellars in which such a large percentage of London's poor are housed, and led us through the brilliant confusion of London street-life at midnight, to the darker alleys where she rescued two children from the cruel treatment of their father.
>
> We observe [in the audience] now a ripple of laughter, now a flutter of handkerchiefs to wipe off a tear of compassion as we listen to Miss Booth's first lesson in scrubology; now again

sobs and tears as she tells us of the matchless heroism of the poor crippled boy who did everything to win an insurance for his starving mother and his smaller brothers and sisters [June 10, 1899].

Soon every city in Ontario—and even further afield—was eager to receive the celebrated Miss Booth in Rags. Nor were they, as this report from the London *Advertiser* attests, disappointed with her performance:

The announcement that Evangeline Booth would speak at the Dundas Street Methodist Church last evening drew an audience that completely filled the large church, many persons standing throughout the evening.

The lecture was Commander Booth's first appearance in London in the costume worn by her among the poor of London, England. She wore a ragged plaid shawl over her shoulders, and crossed in front, and her fingers toyed with the frayed ends as she spoke. A torn white apron half concealed a tattered grey calico dress, from beneath which peeped coarse broken shoes laced with twine. Aside from its immaculate cleanness, the make-up was perfect, and would pass unchallenged in the most squalid court in Old London.

On the platform with the commissioner were Major and Mrs. Southall, Ensign Welch and Willie and Pearl, two pretty little mites, charges of Miss Booth's. Rev. Dr. Saunders, the pastor, opened with prayer.

Miss Booth came forward and sang sweetly an old favourite Salvation Army hymn, accompanying herself on an accordion. Then in a low, pleasant voice she began to speak. Her work was so well known that she needed no apology for appearing in that peculiar garb. Many people wanted to know how she was able to get into the blackest, foulest haunts of vice and crime and poverty in the world and win the confidence of the unhappy people who lived there. Those people hated with a hot, bitter hatred all whose condition was happier than their own, and it was only by means of such a disguise that they could be approached. As a foreign singing girl, or a water-cress girl, Evangeline Booth was able to go among them.

The vital part of Miss Booth's lecture was in the narration of the incidents of her work in the London slums. It would be impossible to reproduce Miss Booth's stories. She lived them over again as she told them. And the audience saw them as if portrayed by some great tragedienne. The sickening brutality, the woeful want, the bitter, burning shame and black despair on those lives came home to the listeners with tearful reality. And then the magic transformation wrought by love and sympathy of one devoted woman was shown.

At times Miss Booth's words came in a torrent of passion and they seemed to choke and burn her; again her speech was filled with poetic fire, as she turned for a moment from the black foulness of sin to contemplate the beauties of nature with a poet's passionate love. There were flashes of playful humour, too, as sunny and careless as a child's laughter. But through it all shone a beautiful, intense, devoted love and sympathy for the poor and suffering. Love, sympathy, sacrifice and action—those were the keys, she said, which had opened to her the hearts of the criminal, the poor and the sorrowful.

The entire lecture was intensely interesting, powerful and dramatic, and the audience listened with almost breathless attention for two hours [July 14, 1899].

Without any doubt, Evangeline Booth was a remarkable and talented lady. She played the accordion and the harp; she was a brilliant elocutionist; and she was, as her biographer makes clear, a consummate performer. She believed, and made explicit her belief, that such talents should be used to win people for Christ. She was therefore not only indefatigable as the Canadian commander—criss-crossing the country from St. John's, N.L., to Victoria in her attempt to promote The Salvation Army—but was imaginatively inventive in her attempts to reach those who remained "just slightly out of reach."

She was, as well, passionate about exercise and the benefits of outdoor activity, even to the point of having a tent set up in her Toronto garden in which she could sleep. She rode her horse as often as possible, and when they became fashionable for ladies, she advocated the healthful benefit of riding a bicycle. Not merely in the city itself, but on long excursions to nearby towns to conduct weekend specials. In the summer of 1897, for example, she formed her first bicycle brigade for a long ride to towns along the road to Hamilton, Ont. As she wrote in *The War Cry*:

> The brigade was timed to leave at 1 p.m., and was formed in line on the ground decided upon for mustering outside the large doors of the territorial headquarters. Eager spectators crowded the windows of Eaton's store opposite, looking with no small admiration upon the neat regulation cycling uniform which by its brown colour appeared to declare the brigade's preparation for the clouds of dust with which during their heated journeyings they would have to contend, and indeed by its close similarity to the earth, seemed to challenge any detection of dirt. Although the customary Army blue was changed to brown, the soldier-cut jacket with braid Ss and epaulettes which mark the military appearance ever accompanying a Salvationist on duty were all in good prominence, and the bugle note announcing the moment of departure combined with the farewell salutes of "God bless you," "Hallelujah," "Pray for us," thrown to the officers remaining in the city, declared beyond dispute that "they went out a band whose hearts God had touched" not for pleasure but for battle.
>
> Staff-Captain Horn and Adjutant Morris formed the advance guard, myself with the two children—Dot and Jai [who Eva had brought with her from England]—on either side, came next in the ranks: then followed the remainder of the brigade in form, each man having his allotted position and specified comrade given by myself, as organizer of the brigade. The uniformity of the parade attracted the attention of all and caused no little comment as it passed through the thronged thoroughfares, for not wishing to run down any

traffic, or wound any quadruped, our speed allowed of our catching the different expressions of wonderment and surprise dropped by onlookers.

"Who are these?" said one.

"Fancy! That looks well," said a gentleman.

"Salvation Army!" cried one or two others.

"Well, what next?—what next?" spoke yet another.

And indeed what next? was the question upon many minds still waiting proof, and other cyclists passing on the way were brought face to face with the fact that you could wheel to heaven with ever so much happier heart and easier propelling than you could wheeling your machine with no greater object in view than your own satisfaction and the whirling away of time [July 31, 1897].

Clearly, Evangeline Booth was enjoying both the sheer physicality of the jaunt and the publicity it generated. During that tour alone, she added, the brigade wheeled over 189 miles, a prodigious feat indeed. The main problem was not the dust but the sun, for the heat was almost unbearable and sunburned skin was a large concern:

However, by rising early in the morning before the elements were well-dressed in fiery brightness, by an arrangement which combined parasol and fan—a flying handkerchief at the back of one's neck, and the aid of an occasional rest beneath a big tree, with a proportionately big bucket of water to quench our thirst, we ran into our specified battle-posts, feeling decided overcomers, certainly having "come through" and "gone over" in more senses than one, no small tribulation.

Then the runs were alike in the kindness that was shown us all along the road. Not only were garden gates, but cottage doors thrown widely open—we could go into the kitchens, despite the dust of our shoes, we could have chairs to sit on under the trees if we preferred, cold water was drawn for us from the well, and in many instances pails of milk were gratuitously bestowed. Tea was offered me by the mother-hearts of a good number of the cottages, the trouble for the preparation of the same being overlooked, and we were even given cake—when I say given, I mean we had nothing to pay for it, which is always a consideration for a Salvationist, and I would like to tell my readers, but I must not, how amused I was in watching how fast the boys could eat it, only of course they had not the least idea how humorously my mind was employed.

Humorously and thoughtfully—the first watching the rapidity with which the substantial square pieces were being disposed of and the latter thinking about the kindness of those who had given it—thinking how it was, just because it is such a beautiful thing to be kind and because kindness, with its deeds and words, never seems able to die, the Master promised exceptional blessing should attend even the giving of a cup of cold water....

We left these halting places a good deal refreshed and rested, but speaking for myself personally, the most beneficial effect was in my heart derived from the fact that as well as those found in the ranks, we had so many who loved us, believed in us, and were anxious to help us in the quiet and by-ways of Canada and since back in the struggle and strife with the regiments of conflicting matters ever trooping through my office, these memories remain to help me.

Renewing her bicycle brigades in the summer of 1889 and 1900—calling them now her Red Crusaders—Evangeline Booth toured most of eastern Ontario, holding camp-meeting revivals. Because the halls were often too hot to be comfortable (and because Eva Booth was a fresh-air fanatic), she rented a large tent, about 15,000 square feet, which was taken by train to the various towns, while she and her bicycle brigade rode the many miles for a stay of about three or four days to conduct religious meetings to which, having heard of her flair for the dramatic, thousands of people flocked much as they would have to the well-known Chautauqua events.

The brigade consisted of about 15 people, divided into four sections: the cyclists, the transport team with the tent, the advance guard which bombarded the towns with posters, and Little Willie and Pearl (her adopted children) who were accompanied by a harp, and travelled by rail. They all dressed in khaki because it did not "show the dust and the material is such as will stand the rough usage to which a tenting party will naturally put it. The trimmings are in red braid, and the black stockings and grey Klondike hats made up a neat and novel uniform."

The first stop, in the summer of 1899, was Deseronto, Ont., in the Bay of Quinte on the shore of Lake Ontario. There they erected their large tent, a feat which, as *The War Cry* put it, offered "excellent physical exercise"—of which Eva Booth thoroughly approved. "There are scores and scores of stakes to be driven with a sledge hammer, and the erection of three masts, and the pulling up of 1,200 pounds of canvas, gives ample opportunity for the full use of muscular Christianity."

And thus began one of Eva Booth's most successful campaigns to which, often, whole communities rallied. From town to town, in such places as Newmarket, Odessa, Colborne, Port Huron, Napanee and Cobourg, Ont., the Red Crusaders became the summer's main attraction. On occasion, Eva Booth would ride her horse (of which she was inordinately fond), while her cohorts rode their bicycles. "Of tumbles there were one or two," wrote a *War Cry* reporter, "but nothing of an artistic or fatal character." But dust-covered they certainly were. "We hope our appearance was imposing as we climbed the Main Street, Newmarket. If we were not as trim as when we started, Yonge Street's sandy hills and dales must be blamed. The dust billows of the roadside had thrown their spray over our uniforms from cap-peak to toe.... The youthful agility and active wheelmanship of Adjutant Welch, Ensign Griffiths and others were somewhat belied by the grey locks upon which their caps rested, dust having done what as yet old age had not given and granted them heads quite remarkable in appearance" [August 5, 1899].

About these summer events, Evangeline wrote to her sister, Emma, that her crusaders had had "regular old Salvation times. The chief object of the campaign was to visit some very small and hard places where the getting of a crowd at all implies that you have the best part of the population out to see you. The people drove in for miles around to attend the meetings, and what with the immense audiences, sometimes stretching outside the canvas, and the almost suffocating heat, the effort was terribly exhausting. [But] we had souls in nearly every meeting, though it almost killed us to get them" [Wilson, p. 125].

In rural Ontario the tent evangelism of Evangeline Booth's Red Crusaders became, for two summers at least, a much-anticipated event. Thousands of Canadians, some Salvationists of course, but many who did not know the Army, were drawn by the sound of the music, by the well-placed posters and the sight of a motley crew of bicycle-riders advancing towards their town. It was an ingenious and effective way of promoting the Army and preaching the gospel, as this *War Cry* report amply illustrates:

> Belleville, our next place of call, is a pretty little town of
> considerable commercial importance. The spot selected for
> the Red Crusaders' campaign here was a broad grassy corner,
> in an excellent situation. The tent went up in fine style. Its
> erection is a science by itself, and the crusaders are getting
> adept at it. Those who are accustomed to lift no heavier
> burden than a pen, may be seen driving stakes, hoisting poles,
> roping canvas, and performing other noble feats of strength
> and skill. In referring to the works department we cannot
> pass over the small boy who has played quite a prominent
> part in it. "Everybody that wants a job, fall in," from the chief

secretary has brought the young hopefuls to stand at attention, and they have reported for some real help, too. At Belleville, Colonel [Read] rewarded his small service corps by some toothsome candies. This early roping-into-assistance of the boyish element has prevented it from becoming a disturbing element during the real business of the campaign. "Now, my beauties, I'll tell you when to talk," from the colonel has had a most peaceful effect, and the behaviour of those who are now generally known as the colonel's beauties, has been remarkably good for their restless and mischief-loving age.

The Belleville campaign was fully on a line with the triumphant events which it succeeded, and the three days spent there will not soon be forgotten. They will certainly wake pleasant echoes in the memories of both visitors and townsfolk. The opening meeting, or, as Brigadier Pugmire terms it, "the preliminary canter," was well attended and enjoyed. Sunday's battle was opened by a knee-drill at which Captain Susie French officiated. The holiness meeting was a time of spiritual refreshing. Brigadier Friedrich, Ensign Hyde and Captain Easton delivered expressive sermonettes, and the colonel gave one of his characteristic Bible readings, which, by their originality and helpfulness, are now so looked for.

A splendid crowd greeted the commander in the afternoon. The event of the evening was her address. It was full of fire and unction, and listened to with rapt attention. Her remarks on cross-bearing were particularly forceful. "I fancy I see some come up to the pearly gates," she cried, "and ask, 'Where is my crown?' and the Master, looking back through your life and work, will ask, 'Where is your cross?' " We have seldom heard the commander more manifestly inspired, and that the Lord owned and blessed her words was seen in the definite cases of salvation which were dealt with afterwards at the penitent form [July 21, 1900].

Inspired by Evangeline Booth's efforts at aggressive evangelism, many of her officers followed her example. During her stay in Canada, travelling specials became a common feature of Salvation Army outreach. As an example, The Salvation Marine Band was started in 1897 by Major Southall, in charge of the Western Ontario Division. Dressed in sailors' uniforms, with "Salvation Army" emblazoned on their hats, they travelled throughout western Ontario in a horse-drawn van—a kind of covered wagon—having been instructed not to travel more than 10 miles a day, "as horses could not be expected to drag the heavy load of bandsmen and instruments farther than that." George Smith, one of the bandsmen, tells how, as an advance guard, he would go into the various towns (Kincardine and Mitchell, Ont., for example) and put on a gramophone recital (that musical machine being then a great novelty), by which he acquired enough money to rent a hall. That was 1897. The next year, still governed by John Southall's ingenuity, the band was re-formed to become an acting troupe, performing a religious play called *The Modern Prodigal*. This they performed in 36 Ontario towns, again demonstrating how, with a little imagination, the gospel could be "taken to the people."

That Evangeline Booth was extraordinarily gifted is beyond dispute; she believed, however, that others, less gifted than she, should use whatever gifts they possessed just as she did. That was how the aggressive evangelism of which her mother had written was to be put into action. And action was her chief delight. Displaying what one writer has called an "irrepressible initiative," she had, while still in London, started one of the Army's first female bands; she was the first Salvationist to ride a bicycle (defying what was then a convention that women did not do that sort of thing); in Toronto she rode her horse to headquarters and slept during the summer, as already mentioned, in a tent in her backyard. She was both innovative and daring; and, by her example, many Canadian Salvationists also engaged in an innovative and daring brand of Christianity.

SEVEN

The Wells' Hill Camp Meetings

Evangelism in God's Garden

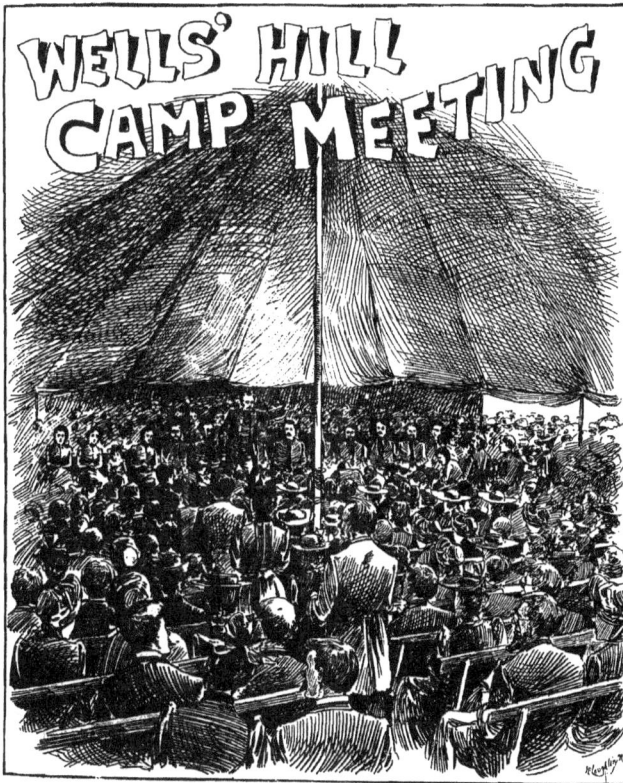

I N THE FIRST AND SECOND DECADES OF THEIR CANADIAN WAR-
FARE, Salvationists liked nothing better than to "gird their
armour" by constant revival meetings. And their favourite,
perhaps the most successful, of such meetings were those of
the summer camp-meeting variety. Not merely ones where they simply assembled for the day, and went home in the evening, but ones
which lasted for two or three weeks, with dozens of tents—a massive
circus tent for the meetings, smaller family tents for accommodation
(at $4 each for the duration) and the important dining tent ("at which
hot dinners will be served every day at 15 cents each").

And, though such camps were held throughout the territory, the
largest and most ambitious—indeed the most celebrated one—was at
Wells' Hill, on the outskirts of Toronto, where for at least eight suc-
cessive summers (1888-1896) thousands of Salvationists, and quite a
few non-Salvationists, from the city and surrounds, enjoyed nature,
shared religious experiences, celebrated weddings and in "four meetings every day" received spiritual nurture and had their soldierly
resolve fortified.

"Among the many beautiful spots that make up the glories of the
northern suburbs of the Queen City," expatiated *The War Cry*, "there
is perhaps none more beautiful in aspect or commanding in its situation than Hillcrest, or as it was known in its earlier days, Colonel
Wells' Hill."

"The view of Toronto that one gets from the precipice," wrote a
Toronto *Globe* reporter, "is probably unequalled, suggesting in its
bird's-eye completeness the view of Montreal from its historic mountain. The altitude sends the eye right across the lake to the Niagara
shore, and Major Margetts strains the credulity of his visitors by
maintaining that he can frequently see the rising spray from Niagara
Falls.... It is a veritable little paradise."

The Wells' Hill estate, a 200-acre farm originally granted to
Ensign John McGill of the Queen's Rangers in 1793 (and then referred
to as Davenport) was purchased from the family by Colonel Joseph
Wells, who served during the Napoleonic Wars, in 1821. When Colonel Wells died in 1853, the land was divided into three long plots, one
of which (the westernmost one, it seems) was bought by William
Gooderham Jr., that devoted Army supporter. It was, as *The War Cry*

noted, the perfect site for an encampment, being just on the edge of the city, atop the escarpment which marks the shoreline of the original glacial Lake Iroquois. It was northeast of the corner of present-day Davenport Road and Bathurst Street, very near where the magnificent Casa Loma now stands. It was here, at the invitation of Mr. Gooderham (and with his full involvement in the meetings), where, with several brass bands, children's choirs, special soloists and numerous speakers, Salvationists experienced "showers of blessings" (and sometimes some of the natural kind as well).

"There were many willing hands," reported *The War Cry* of the first camp (July 31-August 6, 1888), "but the work was by no means light, and for a week the cadets from the lads' home and the Army service corps had been busy making their preparations, and so well and tastefully had they carried out their work, that the grove was transformed into a perfect picture, and a solitary tramp dropping in upon the same might very well have imagined that he had been transported back into the dim and distant ages when knights and paladins took the tented field and did, valiantly, under the red cross pennant. But he would not have been long in being undeceived and awakened to the fact that the modern crusaders were doing doughty deeds and winning victories over the enemies of the cross. The similarity did not, however, end here, for our patient reader will find by the sequel that, as of old, this outdoor tournament and joust of arms as per usual wound up with the usual episode of gallant knight and fair lady [referring, of course, to the hallelujah wedding which ended the week's events]."

Describing the camp itself, the writer maintained his rhapsodic style. "The hillside was covered with tents, large and small, and many city families, Salvation and otherwise, had taken up their abode with the Army for the time being. There were tents for cadets, and tents for officers, the commissioner, Chief-of-Staff, training homes, rescue brigade, and Home of Rest all had their encampments. The monster canvas barracks, which holds 2,000 souls, was all too small for the requirements of the meetings even when eked out by a smaller structure at its side, and the canvas hotel and canteen, on Army principles [meaning no liquor], had hard work at times to accommodate its guests. In the centre of the enclosure, high over all, waved the meteor flag that braves the battle and the breeze, the flag of The Salvation Army, and when at night the huge camp fires threw out their lurid light the scene was at once unique and inspiring, and for far distances their reflection against the sky reminded the inhabitants of the good time in progress and drew thousands to the spot."

With *reveille* at 6 a.m., at the call of bugle, each day began with knee-drill (prayers on the open grass), followed after breakfast by a morning of private devotion and Bible study. Each afternoon and evening there were meetings, some just plain salvation and holiness meetings; others of a special nature such as a Healing Convention, a Commissioning of the Riverside Brass Band, a Salvation Demonstration and Enrolment of Soldiers, a Good-bye, Old Devil, Good-bye Gathering and Exhibition of Saved Drunks and a Grand Musical Demonstration. There was variety to be sure, but there was a consistency of joyful expression and movement ("Colour Sergeant Van Egmond and the commissioner danced an old-time jig"); there were testimonies galore ("One [ex-drunkard] asked all who wanted to know what he used to be and now is to go to his house, stating the street and number, and ask his wife"); the sermons were stimulating (at least, according to the *War Cry* reporter); and many lives were changed.

The special feature of the first Wells' Hill camp, and perhaps one which drew most people to the main tent, was the hallelujah wedding of Reuben Bailey and Annie Salmon. Apart from the actual ceremony itself, performed by the bride's father, Rev. Salmon, the wedding was, as usual, a blend of old-time salvation meeting and a bit of vaudeville. With lots of singing, a host of testimonies (from the bride and groom as well), and plenty of banter, the wedding ended with "three rattling volleys" being fired.

At the end of the first Wells' Hill camp, *The War Cry* evaluated the event as follows: "On Tuesday morning after knee-drill led by Commissioner and D.O. Baugh the camp was struck and the grove left in quietness to glorify God through nature. Space has not permitted us to dwell upon what perhaps to our readers might have been the more interesting side of the proceedings—the many strange things seen and heard, and the amusing, cheering and not altogether uninstructive phases and incidents of camp life. That most were blessed is clearly evident, that all were pleased and enjoyed the time is certain, hundreds who know little or nothing of Salvation circles, and whose only impressions have been picked up in open-airs or occasional meetings, had the opportunity of becoming better acquainted, and the general verdict given is 'they're a proper lot of people, yes they are!' "

In the summer of 1889, the previous year's outdoor sessions having been so successful, The Salvation Army decided to hold two camps, June 29-July 7 and August 1-16. The first was a typical Army revival affair, titled Eight Days' Campaign Against the Devil. "For situation and beauty," wrote the *War Cry* correspondent, "this camp ground cannot be excelled in Toronto. From the top of the hill one looks down upon the Queen City, which scene is made more lovely by Lake Ontario, which forms the background. There is a nice square plot of cleared ground in the centre on which stands the big tent and another smaller one, under which the meetings are held. A beautiful bush surrounds this square plot, and among the trees are dotted the tents of various officers, soldiers and friends, giving the whole a warlike appearance" [July 13, 1889].

Describing the second Sixteen Days' Camp, the Toronto *Globe* had this to say: "During the day there is a good deal of the typical camp ground about the place. Groups sit under the trees on the brink of the cliff and sew, read or chat, as inclination may lead. It is noticeable, however, that when a camper is found reading, it is not a light-coloured brain-freezing novel that he pursues but in almost all cases a worn copy of the holy Scriptures. In the evening large crowds go up from the city and attend the meetings in the large tent under the charge of Commissioner Coombs.... Should you want to spend an hour or more at the camp, the proper plan is, take a Seaton Village car to the terminus of the line and then follow the sign-posted road to the bottom of the hill. As they mount the hill they will probably notice the fine new stairway that has been provided for their climbing" (August 6, 1889).

One special reason for the second camp was to honour Commissioner Coombs, whose farewell had just been announced, and, probably as noteworthy for Salvationists, to dedicate the new Household Troops Band. When the British band of the same name had toured Canada earlier in the year, it had created a sensation among Salvationists and the public alike. As soon as they had left, Commissioner Coombs announced that he would create a similar all-Canadian band and called for volunteers. At the Wells' Hill camp the 18-member band, under the leadership of Adjutant Leonard, inspired the campers with their music, their vocal solos and duets, and gave them reason to be proud when, on the closing Monday, they were commissioned. It was the event of the week and "as they marched into the old tent in their bright new uniforms with glowing enthusiastic faces, what true Salvationist was there present who did not feel thrilled with a present foretaste as well as anticipatory joy of glorious future victories for the Canadian Household Troops Band?"

But it was the glory-filled meetings themselves—filled with song, prayer and testimony—which made the whole Wells' Hill experience memorable. Here is just a sample: "Captain Werry sang, 'Take another look at the cross of Cavalry.' Here the growing enthusiasm almost brought down the platform in the literal fashion. The contagion spread from platform to audience, almost everyone gave a wave-offering. It was a pretty sight to see the white handkerchiefs waving high in the air above the bright red guernseys of the men and the Army 'saints of blue' of the women. 'Only bubblin' up, Major,' said Mother Florence in sweet apology for her irrepressible 'glorys' and 'hallelujahs!' accompanied by an unrestrained dancing for joy in the presence of the Lord" [The War Cry, August 24, 1889].

In 1890, the opening of the summer revival camp—which lasted from August 5 to 25—was described by the Toronto Empire which, from the point of view of vividness, is well worth repeating:

The third annual camp of The Salvation Army was opened yesterday on Wells' Hill, at the head of Bathurst Street, and promises to eclipse its predecessors in many points and ways. The meeting is looked up in Army circles as one of the most important events of the year. It is carried on and conducted by the 13 corps of the Army in Toronto, and is attended by delegates from all over the province. From the experience of the last two years there can be no doubt the idea of holding a camp meeting has been of great use, as the statistics of the Army show that a great many souls have been saved and persons enlightened in regard to the great truth.

A more beautiful spot for camping purposes than Wells' Hill could not be imagined. Towering as it does above the mainland, the view a visit gets of the city and the lake is in itself an attraction, but as it also is the happy possessor of a romantic grove of trees the spot is one of great beauty and value. Scattered in a semicircle are arranged the tents for the officers and men, to the number of 30. Each tent is adorned with the flag of the Army, the colours being yellow, red and blue. A long row of steps makes the ascent to the main entrance to the scene of the encampment a matter of comparative ease. Before the tents are reached a long row of trees are gaily decorated with the flags of the Army and in the evening with lanterns of different shades and colours. The chief tent is known as headquarters and is occupied by Commissioner Adams and his family. The other important canvas coverings are occupied by the sick officers, under the care of Mother Langtry, the Lippincott Home [male cadets] under the charge of Adjutant Matthew, the Yorkville Home [female cadets] under Adjutant Taylor and the canteen under Captain Clarke. Near the later is situated the ticket office which is elaborately decorated with flags and bunting. The large tent in which the meetings will be conducted is situated in the centre of the semicircle, where seating accommodation for 500 persons is provided. Double that number, however, can hear the proceedings of each meeting, as the sides of the structure can at a moment's notice be removed and seats placed alongside those inside. Should a larger crowd be present than 1,000 people, a platform has been erected outside the tent so that an open-air meeting can be held, which will enable everyone to observe and hear the singing, praying and speaking that goes on.

In the rear of the canteen a large tent has been erected, which will be utilized for cooking purposes. Adjoining this is a dining tent, which will accommodate 60 persons at a time. Every arrangement in the culinary line has been made for those who intend tenting out, and apart from the novelty of living in the open air everything will be as comfortable as at home. Every meeting three bands will be in attendance....

In the evening a view of the encampment was one that will not soon be forgotten by those who had the good fortune to witness it. The hill, with its temporary canvas cottages, was a perfect blaze of light. Every tent was illuminated and torches were here and there blazing fiercely. A large crowd of people were, as it was only to be expected, on the grounds, and seemed greatly impressed with the novel scene which presented itself to the eye. The big tent was crowded, and a capital meeting which was led by Adjutant Taylor, took place. It was nearly midnight before silence reigned, and beyond the tread of the guards, which are placed on duty during the dark hours of night, nothing was discernible but the breathing of the sleepers, who, worn out with the heavy day's work, were enjoying a well earned night's rest.

Everything in camp is done in a regular military manner. Knee-drill occurs every morning at 6:30 o'clock. The bugle will sound each morning at 5:55 to rise; also five minutes before the commencement of each meeting to assemble at the tent. The grounds are closed at 10:30 p.m. Lights are put out at the sound of the bugle half an hour later. No singing, prayer meetings or noise are allowed in the same manner as a regular military camp, with the exception that their hours are a trifle longer than those given volunteers (August 6, 1890).

And so, every summer for the next five years Salvationists of the Toronto area looked forward to their Wells' Hill experience, though by 1895 the city was beginning to grow up around them. And it was, as *The War Cry* claimed, "Good indeed! Good in the mornings when the sun bursts forth in glory, when the bugle calls to knee-drill, when the wind whispers peace through the trees, when the heat waves break through the pines in a stream of warm fragrance. Good in the evenings, when the setting sun overflows the camp with floods of red gold. And between the quiet blue and the rosy dawn, soft darkness and the hush of night, with the white tents blanched in the moonlight, all things own him. Doubt vanishes, unbelief seems impossible. Days of pure happiness, days of song and merriment, days of long and beautiful meetings, full of strong-spoken testimony and faltering confession, days of balmy blessing, of spiritual breezes. Sinners forgiven. Pardon and repentance preached by the power of the atonement of our Lord Jesus Christ.... Here, in this 'Colony on the Hill,' one may see how these Christians love one another. Apart from the feverish rush of the sordid world you may study the home life of The Salvation Army behind the scenes, as patent to the eye of day as though they lived, almost, in glass houses. In frank hospitality, 'kindly affectionate,' often sharing all things common in the social community of camp-life" [*The War Cry*, July 20, 1895].

That was, of course, in the usual style of *The War Cry*, a somewhat exaggerated description of the Wells' Hill camp life. But, such idyllism notwithstanding, the rich spiritual blessings of those summer camp meetings must have remained one of the most prominent and pleasant memories for many Salvationists in the late 1880s and early 1890s. And, judging by the vast numbers of non-Salvationists who chose either to attend the special meetings or to camp there all week long, the Wells' Hill camp-meeting experience was one of the Army's more appreciated modes of evangelism.

EIGHT

The Salvation Army at Massey Hall

An Up-Scale Kind of Evangelism

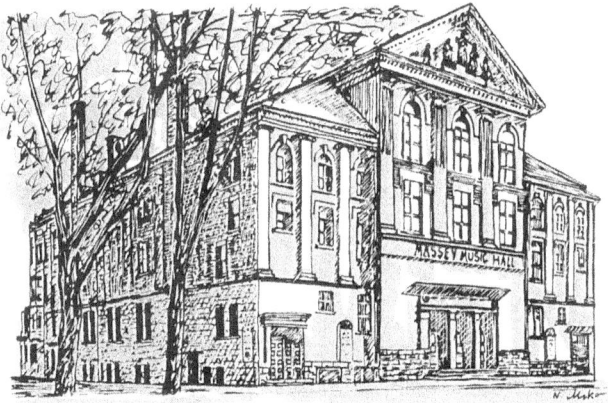

I T WAS JUNE 21, 1894, AND THE SALVATION ARMY WAS PRESENT-
ING its first musical demonstration at Massey Music Hall on
Shuter Street in downtown Toronto.

Just one week earlier, on June 14, a gala performance of Handel's
Messiah, "the greatest musical event in the history of Toronto,"
marked the official opening of the city's new, magnificent concert
hall. The 3,500 seats were filled "with an audience brilliant, fashionable and cultured, who were enraptured not only with the music, but
also with the hall, affording, as it did, the promise of future concerts
of a grade which the lack of such a hall has hitherto practically prevented the people of Toronto from enjoying" [*Globe,* June 15, 1894].

The impressive building, a gift of the wealthy industrialist, Hart
Massey—whose farm machinery was coveted by farmers around the
world—was intended to be, and was soon reputed to be, one of the
great concert halls of the world. Its acoustics, states William Kilbourn
in his history of the hall, were simply magnificent. "A whispered word
could be heard distinctly in the furthest recesses of the gods." The
fact that the 3,500 seats were arranged at three heights—on the
ground floor running right to the lip of the stage, with the curving
first and second galleries above it—and that few seats were more than
90 feet from the stage, contributed a particular power to any
performance.

And that stage, as is well known, was to become the favourite performance space for most of the world's leading musicians and public
speakers. The names speak for themselves: Paderewski, Pablo Casals,
Eleanor Roosevelt, the Dalai Lama, Glenn Gould, Anna Pavlova, Ellen
Terry, Rudyard Kipling, Enrico Caruso, Winston Churchill, Bertrand
Russell, Isadora Duncan. From the New York Symphony Orchestra to
the New Christy Minstrels; from Christmas pageants to labour ral-
lies; from boxing matches to poetry readings, its audiences have been
witness to an amazing array of talent and diversity of performance.

And here, in just its second week, was The Salvation Army, filling
its auditorium to overflowing. If one should wonder why such an
upstart religious organization—one which in the 1890s was still
aggravating the public with its noisy open-air meetings—should have
gained access to such a seemingly high-class concert hall, the answer

is simple. And it was not that the Army, as well as others, could afford the daily $90 fee. It was, rather, that Hart Massey, a staunch Methodist, had decreed that the building would be used not merely for high-brow musical performances but "for such purposes as shall in the judgment of the trustees tend to the musical, educational or industrial advancement of the people, the *promotion of the cause of temperance*, the cultivation of good citizenship and patriotism, or *the encouragement of philanthropic or religious work*, and for the holding and giving of public and other meetings which, in the judgment of the trustees [all committed Methodists], may be consistent with any of the said purposes." The Salvation Army seemed to fit some of those purposes quite nicely.

But let it not be said that those trustees were thereby lowering the tone of the establishment. For it was soon conceded that Salvation Army musicals, under the direction of the talented Herbert Booth, were of a very high calibre indeed; and certainly attracted as large audiences (and not all lower-class, either) as did many of the other so-called classical performers. In fact, using Massey Hall, as the Army did perhaps more than any other organization, except the Toronto Mendelssohn Society throughout its long history, was a means not only of elevating the Army in the public's estimation but of evangelizing a broader and more elite segment of society.

And that was why, just one week after Massey Hall had been opened, The Salvation Army was presenting its first musical demonstration at the conclusion of its annual congress. "Imagine yourself," wrote the *War Cry* reporter, "seated in that crowded top gallery with the platform squarely facing you. Before you is a sight truly magnificent. Looking to right and left and upward the rich-tinted architecture of the Massey Hall first excites your admiration. More electric-lighted fret-worked arches span that lofty ceiling, how beautiful! Yon blue-sky background before which the fretted arch seems to hang like an illuminated cloud in mid-heaven, what an achievement in architectural execution. You turn your eyes downward, past the top boxes with the blue plush upholstery to the sight which meets the eye on the immense platform" [July 7, 1894].

Standing in the central position was Commandant Herbert Booth, waving his baton, as the nearly 500 choristers and 50-piece band sent a wave of musical harmony to the more than 3,000 people seated in the vast auditorium. And when, with that band's accompaniment, the vast audience sang these words to the tune of Sir Arthur Sullivan's *The Lost Chord* ("that marvel of musical beauty" rhapsodized the *War Cry* reporter), it was felt that Massey Hall had truly been dedicated to continued Salvation Army service:

> Oh, Calvary, oh Calvary, the thorn, the crown, the spear,
> 'Tis there Thy love, my Jesus, in flowing wounds appear.
> Oh depths of love and mercy, to those dear wounds I flee:
> I am a guilty sinner, but Jesus died for me.

And then, after a few rousing choruses, the spectacle began. The matrons from the rescue homes, dressed in their distinctive uniforms, sang a pathetic song:

> A little maiden at her mother's knee,
> Emblem of childhood's sweet purity,
> Head downward bending, voice lisps a prayer,
> Safely she's sheltered by a mother's care.
> Little that mother dreams that the years
> Shortly will bring her a harvest of tears,
> Little dreams on some sad future day
> Her darling girl will be drifting away.

> *Chorus*
> Drifting away from mother, drifting away from home,
> Drifting where sins wild breakers, sparkle and
> dash and foam.
> Many a head that's aching under a laugh so gay,
> Many a heart that's breaking, drifting away.

> From that dear mother she went away,
> Life's pleasures beckoning seemed bright and gay,
> Onward and downward she wandered wide,
> Strayed from the right path, a false friend to guide,
> She found the brightness was but a false dream,

Dark, dark as midnight now did it seem,
With her heart breaking, filled with dismay,
Sadly she drifted, drifted away.

And then the Prison Gate Brigade officers presented an object lesson. "A side door of the platform opened, fierce shouts were heard, a poor and apparently hungry man appears, his clothes are torn, in the struggle you infer; he has in his hand a loaf, a police officer in full uniform with his staff drawn has gripped the miscreant, cries of 'stop thief' still re-echo from the corridor, a fierce scuffle ensues, the prisoner goes down two other times, finally the front of the stage is reached, then the prisoner, holding up the loaf turns a piteous look towards the policeman and sings:

Don't run me in, sir,
Don't run me in,
It's only a loaf, sir,
'Taint any sin
Me wife she lies dyin',
The children are cryin',
Don't run me in, sir,
Don't run me in.

At this juncture the officer of the Prison Gate Brigade appears on the scene.

'Give him another chance,' he cries to the officer. 'Let us have him.'

'Why, what can you do with a fellow like him?' says the police officer. 'Who are you?'

'I am the representative of the Salvation Army Prison Gate Brigade; we have a house for the man, and we will find him food, and work and shelter, and give them a helping hand till some permanent situation is found for him.'

'Will you, indeed! Then you shall have him. You can take the loaf and make it into soup, no doubt he is hungry.' Wearing a look of gratitude the prisoner was thereupon marched off ostensibly to the Prison Gate Home, amidst the loudly expressed satisfaction of the public" [*The War Cry*, 1894].

But the crowning piece of the evening was the duet, in the form of answer and reply, sung by Commissioner Cornelie Booth and Lieutenant Ross. The *War Cry* reporter described it this way:

I had made my way to the farthest top gallery when Mrs. Booth's turn to sing came. Lieutenant Ross, of the Lifeboat, took the first part in song 58, and Mrs. Booth replied. Neither wealth, fashion or pleasure, all of which being presented as goals highly desirable of attainment, were sufficient to win the allegiance of "the child of a king," Mrs. Booth's singing is too well known to need any comment here, only that we were glad to note that every word of Mrs. Booth's reply could be distinctly heard at that farthest point, her voice filling the vast auditorium with perfect ease.

The song runs thus:

Lieutenant Ross—
If you had but the wealth of this world as your own,
Oh, what rapture, indeed, you would see;
You could gather all gems, and march through all lore
You could travel all lands, and return with your store,
Oh, how happy a soul you would be.

Mrs. Booth—
Wealth of this world delighting,
Are you my heart inviting?
Richer am I than all your gathered gold;
Farewell! Farewell! Farewell!
I've a treasure untold,
Farewell! Farewell! Farewell!
I've a treasure untold.

Lieutenant Ross—
You could build you a mansion of stone and of gems
With statues, and polished like glass;
You could walk o'er its lawns, and rest in its bowers,

And adorn your apparel with diamonds and flowers
Such as nothing on earth could surpass.

Mrs. Booth—
Fashion and culture charming,
Are you my soul disarming?
Richer adornment do I not procure?
Farewell! Farewell! Farewell!
My robes are pure.

Lieutenant Ross—
You could purchase both pictures and paintings so rare,
 And surround you with children and friends;
And with music and song, and with dance could be gay,
And would fear for no want, and would dread no decay,
And your pleasures would never have end.

Mrs. Booth—
Pleasures on earth enticing,
You have no joy enticing;
Gladness have I, your toys can never bring.
Farewell! Farewell! Farewell!
I'm the child of a king.

That memorable meeting—both to Salvationists and many non-Salvationists alike—ended on a note of triumph with the singing of *All Hail the Power of Jesus' Name*. But it also marked the beginning of many such memorable occasions on which The Salvation Army made splendid use of Massey Hall.

The next occasion was the visit of General William Booth in February 1895. The General had visited Toronto once before, in 1886, but only large churches were available to accommodate the vast number of people who wished to see and hear him. Now, in 1895, when even more people were anxious to hear the "Apostle of the Lapsed Masses," the originator of the world-renowned Darkest England Social Scheme, the new Massey Hall was the ideal venue. And so, at a great reception meeting on February 7, three meetings on Sunday the 10th (one of which was a Toronto temperance meeting), and a farewell gathering on the 12th, Massey Hall again reverberated to the sound of a Salvation Army massed band, a chorus of 250 voices, the joyful clapping and flag-waving of nearly 4,000 Salvationists and friends and, for the first time, the stentorian voice of William Booth.

To get to the hall, however, was a sheer act of dedication. For the weather on that February weekend was at its snow-blowing, face-numbing worst. "The General Conquers a Cold Snap," the *War Cry* announced, and went on to state: "That was what it amounted to—a battle royal between the weather and the reputation and attraction of the General of the greatest religious Army the world has ever known. On the General's side were arranged a vast amount of curiosity, interest, respect, enthusiasm and love. The weather king battalioned regiments of frost—21 below zero—a skinning wind and a mischievous snowfall. In vain the wheels of the tram-cars obeyed the electric current, and whirled round; the rails were ungrippable, and with moanings and groanings, the would-be passengers had to trust to their natural powers of locomotion. A journey of five or six miles under such conditions, with a homeward journey to follow—ugh!!!"

But thousands made the effort. As did Lieut.-Gov. Kirkpatrick (who chaired the welcome meeting), Sir Oliver Mowat (who chaired the farewell meeting), Emerson Coatsworth, member of Parliament, Dr. Withrow, Inspector Archibald, Alderman Shaw and more than 20 other dignitaries and ministers of religion. It was at a time in William Booth's career when public support for his social work was a paramount consideration. Always, therefore, such dignitaries added immensely to the Army's respectability; and Massey Hall served as a perfect embodiment of that respectability. Describing the welcome meeting, the *War Cry* reporter made just such a connection. "The beautiful Massey Music Hall," he wrote, "was a fitting receptacle for such an occasion. Its charms have not been overdrawn. Lightness, loftiness and compactness are leading characteristics.... The colouring—terra-cotta brown, bordered with sunset-blue; the electric illuminants, the two galleries, and all accessories are in harmony, and constitute one of the handsomest and best halls in the world."

In such a setting the General—his physical presence ("high forehead, deep-set eyes, shaggy eyebrows, slightly hooked nose and untrimmed beard"), his verbal eloquence, his apt illustrations—took on an added dimension. Every word he spoke—his depiction of the Army's attempt to alleviate poverty, his arguments against intemperance and his soul-searching sermons—was distinctly heard and every thought taken to heart. There can be little doubt that the Army's decision to rent Massey Hall for the occasion, though not in itself one which determined the success of Booth's visit, went a long way towards according that visit a public prominence which it might never have achieved had it been confined to a smaller Salvation Army venue.

It made sense, then, that for every subsequent visit of the General—in 1898, 1902 and 1907—Massey Hall should be the preferred venue for every major meeting.

In 1898, it was again during a blinding snowstorm—a blast of Siberian weather, said *The War Cry*—that Booth made his Toronto visit (February 3-7) but again the hall was filled. Here is how the Toronto *Globe* described the welcome meeting:

> The night was wild, and the attendance, thought to be numbered by its thousands, was not quite up to the capacity of the great hall, but the General's grip upon his soldiers is as tight as ever. His power of speech, his command of the flashing phrase, his real grace and tact of expression, are with him still, though the years have rolled by, though his frame looks even more spare than before, and though his voice seems a trifle less resonant than before. Most striking of all to the observer, he still has that faculty of marvellous concentration upon the subject of the moment, that fusing together of intense energy with great quickness of perception, which is probably his great characteristic from an intellectual standpoint. His whole frame still seems to sway in the intensity of his conviction and in every respect he is the same leader of men [February 4, 1898].

In 1902 and 1907, William Booth was treated more like a venerated statesman—which, indeed, he had become—than as a travelling evangelist. For many Canadians, The Salvation Army was a highly-respected social-welfare organization, though most knew that its motivation was a religious one. For them, therefore, it was Booth as a social reformer that drew them to the so-called public meetings at Massey Hall. For all Salvationists, however, he was still, first and foremost, their spiritual leader and it was for his preaching, his words of wisdom, that they crowded the hall three times on Sunday.

For example, on Friday, October 31, 1902, it was in appreciation of Booth the social worker that thousands turned out to hear him. "That Massey Hall was so well filled last night," wrote the *Globe* reporter, "was a flattering testimony of appreciation by the people of Toronto of General Booth's great services to humanity and of the great work done by The Salvation Army. The presence in the chair of Hon. Geo. W. Ross [premier of Ontario] was an appropriate recognition of the splendid work done by the Army in assisting the state by caring for and seeking to elevate and reclaim those elements of society which too often become a burden upon the public."

But it was Booth the revivalist who, on the Sunday (both in 1902 and 1907), Salvationists and other Christians came to hear. Again the Toronto *Globe:*

> The three crowded meetings at Massey Hall yesterday testified to the eager interest in what he might have to say, hundreds being turned away from the doors at each service. The enthusiasm of the Salvation soldiers was matched only by the breathless attention with which the vast audiences hung on his every word. His vigour of utterance and of movement conveyed some idea of the energy of spirit that has carried him through 80 years of life, and more than 40 of active campaigning for the Army. His keen thought, his forceful expression and his occasional sallies of wit showed mental powers that give no indication of waning. And the bright optimism, the love of humanity, and faith in God's power and willingness to save the lost, even the lowest, reveal the secret of the wonderful success of his organization, which has outlived criticism and opposition [March 11, 1907].

Without any doubt, William Booth would have met with as

gracious a reception, and have as successfully inspired the people of Toronto during his visits, had his meetings been held elsewhere than at Massey Hall. But, also without a doubt, the fact that the great hall was the venue for both his public and salvation meetings, not only ensured larger audiences than any other could but, in terms of prestige, lent the Army a public credibility no other venue could have. It seemed entirely appropriate, therefore, that when William Booth died on August 20, 1912, the public memorial service in Toronto should have been held at Massey Hall. On August 28, "representatives of national, civic and religious life, and members of The Salvation Army from the humblest soldier in the ranks to the staff-officers and the commissioner, gathered in Massey Hall to take part in the funeral service of General Booth, the venerable Founder of The Salvation Army" [*Globe*, August 29, 1912]. From the lieutenant-governor of the province, to the premier, and hundreds of leading citizens, thousands paid their respects to the dead warrior. "After the benediction had been pronounced, the audience formed up in Victoria Street, and, headed by the massed bands, marched to the city hall square, where the band played a number of the General's favourite hymns. General Booth's picture hung over the main entrance to city hall. The line of march was thronged with people, and many heads were bared as the procession passed."

Massey Hall would echo no more to the gravelly, yet powerful, voice of William Booth. But it would often reverberate to the martial music of Salvation Army bands, the joyful worship of Salvationists and the stirring messages of its leaders and special speakers. Commander Evangeline Booth, during her command of the Army in Canada (1896-1904), gave some of her Miss Booth in Rags performances there, enthralling Toronto audiences. When she was farewelled on November 28, 1904, to take up a new appointment as commander of the United States, her farewell meetings were held in Massey Hall, as were the welcome meetings of her successor, Commissioner Thomas Coombs, two days later.

From almost the moment of its grand opening in June 1894, to well into the 20th century, Toronto's Massey Hall would almost become a symbol of The Salvation Army—as important a means of evangelizing the community as almost any other and, though reaching, perhaps, a more upper-class kind of person, still promulgating the same message of personal salvation as it had to the people of the slums.

NINE

Salvation Army Klondikers

Going Not for Gold but for Souls

WHEN WILLIAM BOOTH MADE HIS THIRD VISIT TO North America in 1898, almost everywhere he went he saw men smitten with Klondike gold fever. He was told of the fabulous wealth to be had in the Yukon where thousands were staking their claims in its gold-fields and some (but not many) were "striking it rich." In the booming town of Seattle, Wash., which he visited on March 7, he reckoned there were as many as 10,000 men, buying their outfits and booking passage for Alaska. As he stepped from his railway carriage, an outburst of enthusiasm greeted him, above the noise of which a big brawny miner shouted, "Klondike or bust, General!"

When the General mounted the temporary platform to speak to the men—"men on the sidewalks, men peering from the balconies and window sills, men impeding the traffic, crowding the Klondike outfitting stores"—he looked over the vast crowd and said to the mayor who had come to welcome him, "This is my Klondike!" And, as the crowd grew silent, he went on: "I am on my way to the Klondike. My Klondike is the kingdom of God. What is yours?" The meeting that followed was a huge success.

In Seattle to meet the General was his daughter Eva, the commander of The Salvation Army in Canada. She was there to escort him on the next stage of his journey into British Columbia. "It was beautiful to meet my dear Eva again," William wrote in his diary, "and find her so much better in health. Like the rest of the world in these parts, I found her full of the Klondike! She is planning for an expedition to save the souls of the miners while they are seeking the gold. God bless her!"

As we have already seen, Evangeline Booth was nothing if not adventurous and innovative. With typical daring she now made the proposal of a Klondike brigade, seeking her father's blessing. "As I have watched crowds of those men," she wrote, "many so young and some old, with songs of pleasure on their lips, descend the gangway of the emigrant steamer, and shout their goodbyes to companions, and as I have also seen them in the over-crowded cars and depots, during my present northwestern campaign, my heart ached with desire to be with them on the field, 'midst the dangers that threaten and the sorrows that await them, to help stem the tides of disappointments and temptations dark and terrible, which are bound to come thick and fast to thousands, and save them by the conquering grace and dying love of Jesus. For what, alas! is before them to relieve the wretched monotony of their lives? Nothing but whisky and gamblers' tables, with all the horrors that follow in the train of these body-wasting and soul-destroying agencies. Although gold abounds, want is dire and painful, for food is scarce, disease is at work and sin is rampant, hurrying on, as always, with its consequences cruel and bitter."

So impressed was her father by Eva's proposal—containing as it did detailed statements of expenses and supplies—and so touched was he by the sight of the prospective gold-seekers in Seattle, that he immediately gave his approval. And, within a month, a Salvation Yukon Field Force was born and yet another means of evangelism had been established. The Salvation Army had, as in so many other instances, seized the moment and responded to a need in a new and innovative way. And the men and women who carried out the mission were acting in the spirit William Booth had intended: "wherever there is a need, go to meet it."

When Eva Booth let it be known, through the Canadian *War Cry*, that she was recruiting men and women for an expedition to "repair the broken dreams of disappointed men," she received many volunteers. It was a new challenge, one which many officers were happy to meet. From the many who volunteered she chose six men—Frank Morris, Thomas McGill, George Dowell, Fred Bloss, John LeCoq and John Kenny—and two women as nurses—Rebecca Ellery and Emma Aiken. They were handpicked by Commissioner Booth herself, who sought people with practical skills as well as platform ability. Thus Adjutant Dowell, a Newfoundlander, was "used to hardships and trials and rough travelling," and could "turn his hand to almost anything"; while Frank Morris was a "first-class cornet and banjo player," and Captain Bloss was "very good on the platform, plays the trombone and sings nicely," but was also a good cook. All were said to be physically fit, a key attribute for anyone intending to climb the Chilkoot Pass. For their destination was Dawson City in the Yukon Territory and would have to be achieved by sheer hard work and determination.

In typical Salvation Army fashion, and in order to raise public awareness and financial support, the Klondike Brigade did not merely board a train to Vancouver and quietly make its way to Skagway. They took a full month to do so—first participating in a giant farewell pageant at Massey Hall and then undertaking a promotional tour which visited more than a dozen cities including Winnipeg and Brandon, Man., Fargo and Jamestown,N.D., Butte, Mont., and Spokane, Wash.

The send-off itself was typical of such events organized by Evangeline Booth—a spectacular, theatrical affair which had Toronto buzzing with interest. Gigantic yellow posters, plastered throughout the city, promised an unusual and perhaps unforgettable evening of Klondike spectacle. And, with the word "Klondike" on almost everyone's lips, it was a packed-out performance.

At eight o'clock, hardly had Eva Booth taken her seat:

... when something—somebody—began to climb the high steps of the orchestra. Could it be a dog? A dog it certainly was, and harnessed to the strangest collection of bundles and bags on a portable sleigh. But who are these? A band of fur-capped, or rather hooded, men, and there are even two women, all looking particularly fit, for there does not seem to be a thin member in the whole party.

Single file they commenced the perilous ascent. Ere this, the almost tiptoeing audience had identified the voyagers as Klondikers, and the steep [stairs] as the Chilkoot Pass. Halfway across a pack, a man nearly vanished over the side and had to be rescued by what looked like Alpenstocks, to the delight of the audience. Reaching the platform on the west side there ensued a great shaking and bustle.

"Well, boys, I'm glad we're over," exclaimed the leader. A few minutes and a tent was up, a hasty meal arranged by means of the most wonderful of folding stoves, and all the accessories of mining bivouac brought out. But the gasping onlookers were still further astonished by the appearance of a portable organ at which an agile Klondiker seated himself and started the strains of—

There's no one like Jesus can cheer me today,
His love and his kindness can ne'er fade away,
In winter, in summer, in sunshine or rain,
My Saviour's affections are always the same.

Which was the cue for Eva to vivify, in her inimitable dramatic style, the terrible suffering endured by the Klondikers as told to her in Seattle and Vancouver. She made people see the suffering, and she talked of the dire need for nursing and medical care, but the commissioner's voice trembled with an even deeper earnestness as she spoke of the spiritual need of godless Klondike—the city which owned no church, could boast no Sunday school, and had neither the guidance of religious influence nor the restraint of social law to hold the wickedness in check. Then turning to the little band of Klondikers at her side the commissioner unveiled the purpose of their costume and the canoes—they were going not for gold, but to meet those two crying needs. Nurses on her right and pioneer officers on her left were to be dedicated to the difficulties, opportunities and triumphs of Klondike Salvationists. The commissioner demolished objections—as to the severity of the climate, well, Salvationists did not easily die; as to the wickedness that was playing such havoc, the attraction and power of the Calvary love was more than a match for that. The commissioner spoke as if inspired until she had carried her hearers to veritably see the suffering and sinning, and the little Salvationist camp amongst them [*The War Cry*, April 30, 1898].

The Klondike Brigade set out from Toronto on April 15, 1898, accompanied by Evangeline Booth herself, but did not arrive at Vancouver until May 12. The month-long trip was spent in promotion and fundraising. In their Klondike costumes (not merely a showy regalia, explained *The War Cry*, but genuine Arctic clothing), the brigade marched through the streets of 12 western cities—in places such as Winnipeg, Brandon, Man., Fargo, N.D., and Spokane, Wash.—preceded by a brass band, while crowds lined the sidewalks to watch and cheer them. At the packed meetings, they performed instrumental and vocal solos, and gave testimonies, before the commissioner gave her now-famous performance of Miss Booth in Rags.

And finally, on May 18, at Vancouver where the SS Tees waited to take them to Skagway, there was a dramatic farewell:

> The comrades and friends filled the space available on the wharf. The passengers already on the Tees lined the rails and when the commissioner knelt on the rough planks of the wharf, hats were removed and in that solemn moment, the commissioner raised her voice and led the vast crowd in the grand old song, "Were the whole realm of nature mine," and at the conclusion Evangeline Booth prayed fervently for the blessing of God upon the officers and soldiers and for the little band of self-sacrificing people soon to brave the dangers of the Klondike Trail. "Goodbye," "God bless you" were called and many other kinds of farewells as the party made their way aboard. Every inch of space aboard the Tees was utilized for supplies being sent to the Klondike. Pens had been built on the upper deck for a shipment of 100 sheep. The stateroom for the commissioner was just below and the bleating and incessant trample on the slippery deck were painful to listen to [*The War Cry*, June 11 and July 2, 1898].

Commander Booth, her personal attendant, Ensign Welch, and the *War Cry* editor, Bruno Friedrich, accompanied the Klondike Brigade as far as Skagway. The trip, as eloquently described by Friedrich, was a memorable one—the magnificent scenery, the introduction to native culture (whose totem poles had not then been carted off by so-called anthropologists), and the obvious possibility of extending the Army's influence. Along the way, the Tees stopped at small villages—many of them combined Indian encampments and commercial salmon-canneries—offering the party opportunities to hold brief open-air meetings and presenting them with a few surprises:

> Our first Sunday after leaving Vancouver will always be pleasantly remembered by all on board. The day had been a

beautiful one, and the sailing most pleasant among the many islands on smooth water. We had a little meeting on board ship in the afternoon which we all enjoyed, and during which a generous collection was given us. The boat stopped at several canneries among the mouth the Skeena River, and at the first place a generous surprise awaited us in the shape of some Indian Salvationists meeting us at the wharf. There was a fine-looking fellow in a red guernsey, some women in uniform, one wearing even a homemade bonnet, S buttons and blue speaking jacket, others having Ss on their collars or badges on their coats. The commissioner was quick to gather them together, to sing a song with them and speak encouragingly to them through a minister on board interpreting for her. It was very touching to watch their dusky faces with wrapt attention listening closely to the commissioner's talk, interrupting occasionally with a fervent "Amen" or "Praise the Lord." The whistle blew, the commissioner prayed fervently for the keeping of those comrades through the inexhaustible grace of God—and away we steamed again.

During the evening we landed at the wharf of Carlisle Cannery, where our boat had to unload considerable freight as well as land some passengers. Here we were compelled to wait for the returning tide before being able to proceed up the Skeena River to our next stopping place. Commissioner was invited by the superintendent of the cannery, Mr. Brewster, whose wife was one of our fellow passengers, to his charming little home, built right upon the rocks, overlooking the broad mouth of the Skeena, bounded by glorious mountains on both shores, while several islands seemingly closed up the inlet. The air was pure and quiet, and the daylight had considerably lengthened, for we had been steaming northerly all the journey. The commissioner played the organ, while the musicians brought their instruments and played them, and we all sang. It was not exactly a formal meeting, but it was a blessed gathering, and I think the angels have put it down in the books as a Service of Song, and called it "good." The passengers and crew crowded into the little parlour and stood on the verandah outside where they heard equally well since doors and windows were all thrown open. The commissioner's voice has been exceptionally well, not only has it been clear and strong throughout all the heavy speaking of the tour, but she has done a great deal of singing, and she did so again this Sunday night. The tenor bass and treble of the party filling in as the occasion required. After a good deal of singing and music which cheered and blessed everybody, [the] commissioner knelt in prayer, lifting up to the throne all those present and those that were represented there in that moment of holiest influence, surrounded by God's handiwork, away from the rush and excitement of the city. It seemed as if heaven was ever so much nearer, and the entrance to the skies so much more accessible to all.

Down we marched: the commissioner playing the guitar and Frank the cornet, as we climbed down the little path, past the Chinese huts, through the cannery buildings and along the wharf to the steamer—and we all felt like Sunday night.

It was after midnight when we reached Port Essington, where we met with a welcome as unexpected as it was hearty. It is true we saw a red-guernseyed Indian standing on the wharf by the uncertain light of a red lantern, but when he disappeared as suddenly as he was seen, we thought we might have been mistaken. We had cautiously climbed up the wharf, and were formulating a plan how to view the village, when we heard it wafted upon the night breeze. What is it?— some familiar tune—listen, listen!—nearer it comes. "Can you make it out, Frank?" one asked. Yes, listen—"His blood can make the vilest clean."

Again and again we hear it—and plainer every time—until we distinguish the tramp of feet, and around the corner they wheel onto the wharf. There they are, Indians in bonnets, in red guernseys and caps, with smiling faces they stand before us, and crowd around the commissioner, who through one of them, who was able to speak English, talks to the leader,

"Committee" Brown, who with gold braid around his cap band and intelligent face, looks the leader.... At the commissioner's request, they sang songs in their native language, followed afterwards by two or three choruses in fair English. Committee Brown informed us that they had a barracks of their own, and wanted the commander to see it. Having sufficient time to do so, we all fell in line, Committee Daniel Brown, leading with his deformed leg and stout stick and loud "Hallelujahs!" Commissioner with her concertina next, our boys with cornets, the Indian Salvationists, and some odds and ends following. In this order we pushed our way along the winding path till we reached the Salvation Army barracks, being the last building in the village right in the woods. The structure is a very creditable one in every sense, well proportioned and braced up, properly shingled, with an ascending platform, the arches of the windows having coloured panes of yellow, red and blue glass, and it displayed an experienced carpenter's work and ingenuity. There were tambourines as well as a fine drum and homemade flag.

The commander sang and played the concertina and afterwards spoke to the others, one of the Indians interpreted for her, exhorting them to purity of life, singleness of aim and goodness—putting everything in as simple language as possible—to love each other, to pray for their adversaries and let their lives be an uncontradictable testimony to the change which they claimed to have experienced in their hearts.... With hesitating steps we went back through the night to our boat, our thoughts still lingering with the little quaint barracks in the woods, and our ears still resounding with the song from the lips of our dusky comrades: "His blood can make the vilest clean."

On May 27, more than an eventful week after leaving Vancouver, the Klondike Brigade arrived at their final departure point—Skagway, Alaska, a boom-camp situated at the northern end of the Lynn Canal. As an Indian summer fishing camp it had been both quiet and beautiful; as a gold-rush terminus it was "conceived in lawlessness and nurtured in anarchy" [Pierre Berton, *Klondike* (1958)]. Crude saloons and dance halls were open round the clock; vagabonds roamed the streets; murders were not infrequent; and the whole town, so some historians say, was subject to the dictatorial whims of the notorious criminal Soapy Smith who was killed by a vigilante committee just five weeks after Evangeline Booth's visit.

At least two of her biographers insist that Evangeline Booth met Soapy Smith and that they sat, drank cocoa and talked about spiritual matters for hours. "Amid the shadows of the forest," writes P.W. Wilson, "they prayed together and Soapy Smith departed" [*General Evangeline Booth* [1948]: 129]. Unfortunately, no evidence is provided to support such a claim, and none seems to exist. In the detailed, and ample, report of her three-day stay in Skagway, in which one would expect to find a mention of such a notable meeting, there is none. The only mention of Soapy Smith made by Bruno Friedrich, the *War Cry* editor, who was there with her, is that he did begin the collection by dropping $5 in the basket. In spite of the lack of any definite meeting with the notorious Soapy Smith, there was still much to occupy Commissioner Booth and to make her stay, though brief, both exciting and productive:

> What a motley crowd stood there on that narrow wharf, stretching over 2,000 feet through the shallow water to reach a safe landing place for ocean steamers. Presently a man dressed in a corduroy suit, jumped on deck and presented himself to the commissioner as a London newspaper man who had been in some of her meetings in the world's metropolis. No sooner had we stepped on the wharf than a driver stooped down from the seat with tears in his eyes and voice to shake hands with Miss Eva Booth. Up we went through the roughly laid out streets, lined with unique frame buildings, till we reached the narrow entrance of the [Chilkoot] trail, where only picturesque log shanties are erected anywhere between stumps and fallen timber, and the little brook is picking its way through the brush and branches and broken limbs. Here we decided to pitch our tents, and a

gentleman cheerfully offered us his ground, telling us, with visible emotion, how he had heard the commissioner two years ago at Spokane. The next building was inhabited by a neat German woman, who gave the commissioner the freedom of her one-roomed, but scrupulously clean hut, and we believed her husband when he told us that he had been living up there all winter by himself, "but now since the wife has come I am happy as a king."

There was plenty to do; the boys went back and forth getting their baggage, and passing goods through the customs, as well as attending to numerous other errands. Commissioner personally purchased the food for our meals, and considering the fact that this was probably a very unaccustomed business for her, she managed the commissariat admirably well, and made a very happy selection. There was corned beef, fresh butter, nice bread, canned fruit, tinned salmon, fresh lemons and tea. A happy and enjoyable meal we had together. Commissioner would not rest till she had explored the length and breadth of Skagway, the inside and outside of stores, and had been a couple of miles up the trail. The wonderful lightness of the air made walking rather a pleasure, and so it happened that Miss Booth was not in such a fatigued condition as she would have been otherwise, when the time for the open-air arrived.

The spot selected for our meeting was right between some of the most noted saloons—the Pack Train saloon on the one side, and Jefferson Smith on the other. This being the most frequented part of the town, a tremendous crowd soon gathered and blocked the street. Of course they were almost all entirely men; they crowded close upon the ring, they stood on the sidewalk, they hung on to the sign posts, and were seen standing on barrels and boxes and anything that had the advantage of some elevation, and could be observed through the open door of the saloon standing on the counter inside. Men on horseback halted on the outskirts of the crowd, and the upstairs windows of one or two buildings which had an upstairs, were crowded with spectators, but they all listened with the closest attention.

The crowd of curious Klondikers were especially delighted—as were all crowds along the way—to hear Thom McGill's *Klondike Son*, sung to the tune *We're Going Back to Dixie:*

> When the General was in Seattle
> Amid the noise and smoke of battle,
> His heart went in pity for the North.
> The commissioner took in the situation,
> And arranged this expedition;
> So we're off to the Klondike for all we're worth.
>
> *Chorus*
> We're going to the Klondike (repeat);
> We're going after sinners in that land;
> We're happy lads and lasses,
> We're not afraid of passes,
> We're going to the Klondike at God's command.
>
> Here's Dowell, an old-timer,
> And Kenny, he's a climber,
> Lecoq and Bloss have been men o' war;
> McGill is an old farmer,
> And Morris, he's a charmer,
> And Ellery and Aiken are all there.
>
> There's lack of woman's nursing;
> There's lack of woman's tears;
> A famine of their love and tender care,
> So open up your purses,
> Assist those two brave nurses,
> Who for Jesus' sake are going right up there.

No doubt one would have had to see this performed, with appropriate nods to the proper people, and a bit of vaudeville showmanship, but we are told the crowd thoroughly liked it, as one in the crowd called for three cheers for the Klondike farmer. "The cheers were not only heartily given, but in a very practical way by a shower of silver dollars and other smaller pieces, amounting in a very short time to nearly $33."

When the commissioner rose to speak, she was greeted with quite an encouraging applause. She selected as her theme, "Thou shalt call his name Jesus," and at considerable length held the immense crowd spellbound. She frequently sang— for her voice has never been in better tune since coming to Canada, and her songs clinched the conviction that had smitten many a heart. They not only listened eagerly, but they literally drank in her words. Such a crowd as they were—they must be seen to be at all appreciated—the old men and the young men, the learned and the shrewd, and the brutish one, the one well-to-do but now dissipated, the once poor but now rich, the gambler, the honest prospector, the tenderfoot just arrived from the east—they all were there in their broad-rimmed hats, their blanket-jacket or dunnage coat, or corduroy suits, leggings and heavy boots, and their belts suggesting the revolver—they had come from Sweden and Norway, from Great Britain, France, Italy and Germany, from Mexico and Australia, even from Africa—a more cosmopolitan and picturesque crowd you have never rested your eyes upon. Most of our ship's crew were there, too—last, but not least to be mentioned, for right stout-hearted and brave fellows they were. But they all as one listened with breathless attention. Oh, that you could have seen the twitching of faces in vain attempt to check the uprising tears and conceal the better emotions rising in their hearts—but they failed, first a tear here and there was wiped off shamefacedly, but soon that was forgotten and many were seen crying—yes, some were crying piteously, especially two women of questionable appearance who broke down altogether, hiding their faces in their garments, when the commander knelt and started the old chorus:

Home, home, sweet home,
There's no friend like Jesus,
There's no place like home.

But men gave way similarly—old men crying like children—and the meeting stamped itself indelibly upon the minds and consciences of that Skagway crowd. It will always remain a restraining memory in days of darkness and temptation and doubtless prove the turning point in the lives of many.

When Eva Booth returned to Vancouver on May 28, the focus of the venture returned to the Klondike Brigade itself. Their first task was to climb, with all their equipment, the forbidding Chilkoot Trail, and then it was to hike, canoe and portage 500 miles down the Yukon River system to Dawson City. It was there the seven Salvationists would establish their "mission of mercy" to the thousands of Klondikers who crowded its narrow confines.

The first of these challenges was the Chilkoot Pass itself, a 35-mile trail crawling upward through a narrow gorge, the last steep climb of 45 degrees through a trough of ice and snow. "There were only two points on this four-mile stretch," writes Pierre Berton, "where a climber could properly rest. The first lay beneath a huge over-hanging boulder which, because it afforded some shelter, was known as stone house. The second was a flat ledge only a few city blocks square at the very base of the final ascent, known as The Scales because everything was re-weighed here and the packers' rates increased to a dollar a pound. Loaded animals could go no further, even sleds and dogs had to be packed over on men's backs" [Ibid, 249]The trail itself, which saw as many as 30,000 Klondikers brave its dangers, was, even by the time the Army's Klondike Brigade set foot on it, beginning to be littered with dead horses and mules, and was proving to be the heartbreak of many would-be miners. "It would be a hard heart indeed," wrote Frank Morris, "that could pass by the poor animals tugging along up the mountain steps with loads far too heavy for their endurance as witnessed by the numerous skeletons to be found all along the trail." To be certain that those who started out had a chance of reaching the summit, the North West Mounted Police demanded that each Klondiker pack a ton of supplies so as not to be left destitute on the trail. But, even with such precautions and with Indian packers to help, many did not make it to the divide. That the Klondike Brigade did, and did so without mishap, is a tribute to their fitness and dedication.

It was also a tribute to the respect and goodwill they had already achieved. "It would be wrong," continues Morris, "to give the impression that only men with hard hearts and cruel hands exist, or that this is a region where only thieves and robbers thrive. Already we have seen scores of beautiful spirits; in fact, such seems to be in the majority, even amidst surroundings which are often peculiarly adverse. These admire the Army, and the fact that we are officers in it elicits for us great courtesy and willingness to assist and help us in any way."

It was, nevertheless, a demanding climb—"sometimes with all hands and feet, and at others managing to make slow progress by means of a walking stick. Still, we got there—got right on the summit, and although when we landed it was blowing a frightful hurricane and you could hardly see 10 feet in front of you, yet nothing daunted, after attending to our effects, we began to descend. I will not attempt to describe how, but suffice it to say anyhow, with 70 pounds on our backs we did it, and went first across Crater Lake, then through the canyon and later to the further end of Long Lake in a thick fog, frequently sinking through the slushy snow to the thigh. But we stuck to it, and seven miles of the worst walking which could be imagined was overcome."

It was not enough to walk over the divide, however; the canoes and provisions which had been transported to that point had to be retrieved and brought down as well.

"Tomorrow morning," the adjutant said, "we must begin to pack our stuff down from the summit." Bright and early (and it seems always early here, as it never gets dark), through deep snow over the still frozen lakes and canyon the party hurried toward the summit, passing innumerable dog-trains and packers on the way. Our destination reached, one of our large canoes, containing an extra 300 pounds was put on small sleighs, and then the haul began. Reader, imagine yourself with five others tugging away at a big boat through countless snowdrifts, with at least every 10th step sinking in to the knees, sometimes pulling up grade at an angle of 50 degrees. As you may experience a great variety of temperatures and conditions in a few hours here, this work has to be done at times through a dense fog, at others in a snow storm, and again beneath a furious sun which has the power to scorch and burn up your flesh in a fearful manner— such had been the experience of each member of the Salvation Army Klondike Expedition. Nevertheless, as the old adage has it, "there is a silver lining to every cloud," and while we only succeeded in getting the first canoe five miles in one day, the next brought a wonderful change in the right direction. Having secured two good sleighs, a sail was soon hoisted and a terrific gale blowing in our favour, when once started we sped along with magnificent speed, so the full seven miles were covered in less than two hours.

This done, our entire outfit was landed this distance beyond the summit in three days. "You fellows beat all creation," was the expression of one individual, and why should we? We are going to the Klondike for a righteous cause, and God is with us. It is a remarkable thing (and not so remarkable, after all), at every turn things have turned in our favour—on all sides we are treated with courtesy, kindness and words of cheer [*The War Cry*, July 9, 1898].

Nor did the Salvationists forget why they were making this trip, and, in spite of sore muscles and tired limbs, they held open-air meetings whenever possible. At Lindeman, at the south end of Lake Lindeman, where Klondikers had erected a small tent city at which to prepare for the next stage of their journey, they conducted two "splendid" meetings, "crowded with eager and appreciative listeners, all of whom gave us the warmest of welcomes. The moment the cornet sounded and the singing commenced the people emerged from the sea of tents, and in a few seconds more they had closed around us and the meeting was in full progress. Rough-looking men, it is true, they were who stood around that ring, but nevertheless with hearts as the pearl encased in the rough shell, and not so hard either as their circumstances and environments might be considered to make them, as indicated by the tear as it stole out of the corner of the eye and brushed hastily away ere it was noticed. Spontaneous offerings amounted to $19.20" [Ibid].

The first challenge having been met, the next lay in assembling the canoes, crossing the lakes—Bennett, Tagish and Marsh—which lie at the headwaters of the Yukon River, and then navigating the dangerous waters of the Yukon itself. The notorious Squaw and White Horse rapids had, in the preceding year, played havoc with more than 200 boats and had taken many lives. And while at this time (June 1898) members of the North West Mounted Police were checking boats for safety, making women and children walk around the rapids, and allowing only knowledgeable men to take boats through the gorges, it still remained an arduous and perilous trip:

> We made 65 miles yesterday [Saturday, June 18], and came through Thirty-Mile River which was the most dangerous part of the route today. In some places the current runs at seven miles an hour. I don't think there was any point where we could see a mile ahead; it was one turn after another, and around nearly every turn there were rocks in the river....
> Around a sharp turn we came on eight or 10 men standing on the shore throwing ropes out into the water. They called to us to save the man they were trying to help. He was clinging to a rock about 60 feet from shore—his boat had been wrecked— but the water was running so swiftly we could not reach him. Our boat went to shore below the rock, the other landed up above. The men waded out as far as they thought safe and threw the wrecked man another rope but he was afraid to let go of the rock. He had been in that plight for half an hour before we arrived. Just as our boys called to him to grab the rope, another boat was drawn by the current close to the rock. Then Adjutant [Dowell] shouted to him to jump to the boat. He did and caught the back paddle. He could not be pulled in but he got a grip on the back of the craft and was

towed to shore. Of four men in the shipwrecked man's boat, one had drowned and two had clung to the boat. Three boats were wrecked that morning, five the day before.

Landed at Salmon River about eight o'clock. Did some washing, tended to other duties. It was 12:15 when I went to bed and it was still light. It is so hard to get enough sleep. There are 30 men camped at this place, all going to Dawson City. Three Mounted Police live there and check every boat that goes through. Everyone has to report so that if a boat is lost they know by the name and number who were in it. We reported first at Tagish Lake and have reported four times since. It must be very lonely for the Mounties. They live in tents at present and are building log cabins for the winter. Just fancy! We've not seen one house or one person living along the route since we left Skagway—only those who, like us, are going through, camping for a while, picking up and going on again. We have come about 300 miles and have about 180 more to go before we see Dawson—all the way by water ["Saga of the Klondike," *Canadian Home Leaguer* (1972-73)].

On June 25, 1898, the Klondike Brigade reached Dawson City and found itself in the midst of what seemed like a garish carnival. Tents and shacks crowded every inch of space, and thousands of frenzied gold-seekers thronged its muddy sawdusted streets. "When we got to Dawson," writes Ensign McGill, "we got the most amazing welcome. I venture to say about 500 men—hardly a woman in sight—crowded on the main street, which was sawdust, and they lined the river bank. They clapped and cheered and did all they could to assure and reassure us we were welcome, and a beautiful sacred influence pervaded the whole meeting. Why! The first collection was something like $70."

Dawson City was, at that moment, the largest city west of Winnipeg, with a fluctuating population of between 18,000 and 30,000 people. "Only about one half of this number bothered to look for gold, and of those only 4,000 found any. Of the 4,000, a few hundred found gold in quantities large enough to call themselves rich. And out of these fortunate men only the merest handful managed to keep their wealth" [Berton, 417]. Thus, the streets of Dawson City were filled with thousands of aimless men, many without the courage to return home empty-handed, more with no money to do so even if they wished, imprisoned in a town of false-fronted saloons where whisky was cheaper than wholesome food.

Determined to help these men, physically as well as spiritually, the seven Salvationists set to work. They went up river to cut logs, floated them to a site and built a residence, a barracks and a shelter for the men they would serve. Soon, in the words of the San Francisco *Chronicle*, there were "long lines of stranded and sick gold-seekers. The shelter is filled to capacity. Applicants who are physically able are required to pay for bed and meals by sawing wood which is in great demand" [February 4, 1899]. The services of Ensign Ellery and Nurse Aiken were especially appreciated, and never more so than during the frequent outbreaks of typhoid and scurvy.

In accepted Army tradition, the whole operation was financed locally: no money whatever was received from territorial headquarters. In an area where a gallon of milk fetched $4 and where it cost a thousand dollars to feed a horse for one winter, this was not an easy task. There were buildings to raise, supplies to buy ("Butter costs $1 per pound, eggs $2.50 a dozen," wrote Ensign Ellery) and men to feed and clothe. Collections, therefore, were always uppermost in their minds:

> There are crowds of people here, more than will ever be able to leave and they are still coming. Hundreds would leave if they could get out. The gold is very plentiful in some places, but everyone can't get it. Gold dust brings $14 per ounce. The people have given us over $600 since we arrived. I collected from the saloons and hotels about $50 and not one word was said to me that was out of the way.... Last Monday Ensign Morris, Captain Bloss and I started for the mines at the Forks. Got in around nine o'clock at night after walking about 16 miles over a very rough trail, over streams of water and sluice boxes. Very tired when we arrived. I had a cabin to myself a little way from the men. Tuesday I collected at the mines. Not

many attended the meeting we held; hardly anyone knew we were there. A miner stepped into the open-air ring and gave me a cigar. Wednesday we visited other mines. Some were panning out well; others were not. One man panned $800 and gave me $5 worth of gold dust. Thursday, Ensign and Captain went to see brother Halfly, while I collected around the Forks. In a saloon two young men treated me to a glass of lemon. When I called at a neat little cabin where a miner lived he asked me to stay and gave me the best meal I have had in this country. Stayed all night with a German woman. Next morning the boys called for me and we walked back home, getting in at eight, pretty tired [Ellery, "Saga of the Klondike"].

From such accounts we know that the Klondike Salvationists endured considerable hardships and ministered devotedly to the miners of the region. We cannot, of course, know the full extent of either their hardship or devotion, and know only that it was one of those occasions when The Salvation Army recognized a need, worked diligently to meet it, and when that need no longer existed, withdrew to tackle yet others. For, in just three years, the Klondike gold rush was, to all intents and purposes, over. The gold had petered out, and Dawson City's population, more than 22,000 in 1901, dwindled to about 4,000 by 1914. The Salvation Army closed its doors in 1912, long before Dawson City became famous as a tourist attraction. It was one of those rare moments when the soldier of fortune and the soldier of Christ met to provide an experience in which fact is as strange as fiction.

TEN

Evangelizing in the Face of Death

Canadian Salvationists in the First World War

T O EVANGELIZE IN THE SLUMS OF DOWNTOWN TORONTO, OR even in the remote mountains of British Columbia, might have been challenges most committed Salvationists were willing to meet. But to make one's religious convictions manifest in the trenches of a war zone, and even attempt to evangelize one's fellow soldiers, might have seemed an action beyond the call of duty. Many Canadian Salvationists, however—thousands of whom became soldiers in khaki in the First World War—did just that. They did not leave their religion at home but took their enlistment in the Canadian Expeditionary Force as yet another means of promoting, by deed and word, the gospel they adored. In the preparatory camps, and in the trenches of France, young men—many of them Salvation Army bandsmen—displayed their colours just as they would have in their barracks or on the streets.

In the many histories of the First World War, when The Salvation Army is mentioned (which is only rarely), it is mainly to say how appreciative Canadian soldiers were of the services the Army provided by way of leisure hostels and canteens. Salvation Army huts were places where soldiers, taking a rest from trench warfare, could have a hot drink, write letters home or gain an ear to have a personal chat, even about spiritual matters. For, in addition to the Salvationists who had volunteered to staff those huts, there were several official officer-chaplains—men like Adjutant Robert Penfold (the first official Salvation Army chaplain), Captain Alf Steele, Adjutant C.B. Robinson and Adjutant Carroll—who looked after their men while they trained in England and went with them to the front lines in France. Theirs was not merely, as some historians would have us believe, a continuous round of dispensing hot coffee, but an on-call routine of personal counselling, church parades and burial services. Here is one of Adjutant Robert Penfold's frequent reports to the Canadian *War Cry* in October 1916:

> I started my work here in an old dugout in the bank by the
> side of the road with a roll of tar paper to cover it, and
> supplied hot cocoa, biscuits and chocolate, etc., to the men. A
> little later I added an addition composed of material I
> managed to forage and which comprised tin-biscuit boxes,

rubber sheets, tar paper, chicken wire, poles and boards. Up at the front here it is difficult to get material, and you have to do the best you can. I have now managed to purchase a good-sized marquee, and have put in writing paper, reading material and games, and have fitted it up with tables and seats, so that it is good and comfortable for the men.

I have had the sad duty of burying the first man of our battalion who has been killed since coming here. He was buried in a cemetery a short way behind the firing line. It was a most impressive event, and one that I shall not forget. The cemetery is beside the main road leading up to the trenches, and while the service was going on the road was thronged with traffic, going up to and returning from the firing line. The great push was on, and fresh troops and supplies were being rushed up to the firing line, while the men who were being relieved were coming down and being cheered by their comrades going in. The ambulances were screaming down with the wounded, and at a temporary dressing station just in front of us three German prisoners were having their wounds attended to.

A little to our left a battery of our big 9.2s were blazing away and making the very air quiver with the concussion from their reports. One of our new armoured cars or "tanks" as they are called was drawn up on the side of the road looking like some huge prehistoric monster waiting to devour anyone rash enough to approach it. I can well understand the terror of the enemy as these huge machines come lumbering across No-Man's Land, crawling in and out of shell holes and mine craters, climbing over their parapets, and stopping at no obstacles, even crushing down trees and going right through houses when necessary. To see them in the darkness spitting fire as they came and taking no notice of the shot and shell that were being rained upon them, must have been a most awe-inspiring sight.

However, these sights which interested us, have ceased to have any attraction for the brave lad whose body we are committing to the earth, and whose soul we are commending into the hands of his Maker. We place a neat cross over his grave and leave him until that hour when "the dead shall hear the voice of the Son of God, and they that hear shall come forth to the resurrection of the just."

As I write these lines I am sitting out in the open, and from our camp we have a beautiful panoramic view of the surrounding countryside. It is a lovely, bright Sunday afternoon, reminding me of our Indian summer in Canada. Directly in front of me is the town of Albert, from which every little while a huge cloud of dust and smoke arises as a German shell explodes. Away to the right is a magnificent valley, through which a fine tree-bordered road runs. The ground is dotted with encampments of the various units, and presents a most spectacular sight. Away to the left they are just hauling down a "sausage" balloon, which has been doing its work as one of the eyes of the army. Truly, "every prospect pleases and only man is vile." ...

[Later]: I have thought you might be interested in a description of one of my church parades up here at the front, so will try and give you an idea what they are like. It is a beautiful Sabbath morning, with the sun shining brightly and just enough breeze to keep the air from becoming oppressive. In fact, just like an August day at home, and unconsciously our thoughts turn to dear old Canada, and we feel a bit of a tug at our heartstrings as we think of our comrades and loved ones, and wonder how they are getting on and when we shall see them again.

Across the road from our camp there is a large field with quite a depression in the ground. The colonel has wisely chosen this for parade purposes as the men can assemble here, and, when formed up, their heads are only on a level with the road. The advantage of this is quite obvious as they are safe from observation from the German kite balloons, or sausages, as they are more familiarly known. It also makes it more difficult for the enemy aircraft to spot them.

As there are no working parties out today, the whole battalion, including all the officers, are present, and are formed up in front of a little bank, on which the colonel and I take our stand. All the men have their gas helmets and carry their rifles, as they must be prepared for any emergency up here so near the front line. From the place where I am standing there is a very interesting view which I shall try to describe.

Directly in front the ground slopes upward and spreads out into a large fertile Flemish farm. The farmhouse and stables have miraculously escaped being shelled, but the solid brick building leading over the little stream to the stable has a large hole in it where a high-explosive landed and went right through it into the water. The ground has produced an abundant harvest, and a considerable portion of the grain has been cut and is standing in stooks. The balance is waiting for the reaper. The hop fields stand out very distinctly in their rows of vivid green against the golden glory of the ripened grain.

There is also evidence that another reaper besides the Flemish farmer has been busy in these fields, for, dotted here and there are the little wooden crosses which indicate the fact that several brave men have made their final bivouac and are awaiting the reveille of the resurrection....

Immediately behind where I stand the main road leads up to the front. Along this the panorama of war is continually unfolding itself. Here the motor lorries with all kinds of supplies hurry on their way to try to satisfy the insatiable appetite of an army at war. Huge guns lumber by to take their part in the conflict, while men on horseback, on foot, and riding bicycles or wagons, are continually coming and going. Every once in a while an ambulance car will scurry by on its mission of mercy.

But it is time for the service to commence. The hymn is announced and the battalion band that I have secured furnishes the music, and the words of the grand old hymn, *O God, Our Help in Ages Past*, is sung lustily by the men. After asking the blessing of God upon us, and not forgetting the loved ones at home, we have another hymn; the Scripture lesson is read, and we sing again.

As we sing we hear the anti-aircraft guns open up and the shells burst in the air away to our right. It is one of the enemy planes trying to get over our lines for observation work. I note that the officer commanding and some of the officers are anxiously scanning the sky; but the would-be raider is driven off.

Fritz has been remarkably good today, as Sunday is usually chosen by him for heavy "strafing"; but it has been very quiet indeed. And now for a short time I address the men. As I face this large number I lift up my heart to God for the right message that will be a means of blessing and of leading them to him. The address finished, we sing *Lead, Kindly Light*; the benediction is pronounced, a verse of the national anthem is sung, and the parade is dismissed, and I hurry off to conduct another parade at the other camp. I trust you will find this a little interesting, and I will write you again, as soon as I can make time to do so.

Without question, the contribution made in the First World War by Canada's Salvation Army chaplains cannot be overestimated. Along with other official services provided by The Salvation Army—the many canteens and huts, the 17 motor ambulances, the thousands of mitts and stockings sent to soldiers, and the comfort given to widows—they represent a considerable wartime effort. It was, however, only one feature of The Salvation Army's presence in the war zone. The several thousand ordinary Salvationists (soldiers, adherents and officers) who enlisted and served in the Canadian Expeditionary Force, in the trenches at Flanders or Ypres or Courcelette, also made the Army's name known and its evangelistic mission evident in their personal conduct and their concern for their fellow soldier's spiritual welfare. With their red guernseys worn beneath their military uniforms, or their Salvation Army badges proudly displayed, or with song book and Bible, and often with the brass instruments they had brought along, they often became the unofficial chaplains of their battalion or brigade. The same brand of evangelism they had practised in their home corps they now practised in the front-line trenches.

"Say, boys! Supposing we have a sing-song to buck us up!" The speaker was one of 120 Canadian lads in khaki who were billeted in a war-wrecked church "somewhere in France." The roof and walls of the edifice—what there was left of them—let in alike the sunshine and the rain and occasionally shells!

The suggestion was adopted at once, and there were shouts for the eight Salvationists who were among the company. Four of these, who had been bandsmen in the Land of the Maple Leaf, had brought instruments with them, and these were quickly got out, song books were distributed, and in a few moments a rattling Salvation Army meeting was in progress.

How those men sang, *There is a Fountain Filled With Blood*—never had some of them thought of it until now; *Abide With Me*—yes, they would need him, for "we may be attacked at any time"; *Nearer My God to Thee*—ah! That was what the Salvationists were striving for, to bring those men nearer to God. Nor were their efforts in vain.

Presently one who had been standing dropped on his knees in the straw and quickly a Salvationist was at his side, praying with him and pointing him to the Saviour. Soon there was another and yet another, until six were kneeling there seeking salvation [Canadian *War Cry*, February 19, 1916].

II

Salvationists will not be done out of their meetings— wherever two or three of them are located meetings invariably follow. In one battery of the Royal Field Artillery there were six Salvationists who became much exercised about the salvation of their mates. After holding a little council together they decided to have open-airs at least three nights a week when duty permitted. Night after night they formed their little ring behind their guns in true Salvation fashion, gave out their songs, and testified to the men of the power of God to save and keep from sin.

At first some scoffed and others stood off, but very soon all became very deeply interested, and at the sound of the voices of the Salvationists would gather round and stand with caps off while prayer was offered, and then heartily join in singing such grand old salvation songs as Lead, *Kindly Light, Rock of Ages* and *There is a Fountain*.

"We used to have meetings," said one, "whenever possible. Two or three of us would get together in the trenches and sing; our fellow soldiers would come around—when there was a lull in the fighting—and all would join in. The favourite song was *Nearer, my God, to Thee*. At times we would be within 30 yards of the enemy's trenches, so they could not fail to hear us singing. If there was time, we would have testimonies and read the Bible. But more often than not our little meeting would be disturbed by the 'Jack Johnsons' or some such gun, and the bursting of shells in or near the trenches would recall us to our work of defence."

There are some stirring stories connected with the singing of Salvationists on the battlefield. In one of the early battles a battery of artillery was ordered to follow the retreating Germans. In doing this six of the soldiers got lost, amongst them being a Salvationist, and for four days they were tramping about without a mouthful of food or drink. This is the story as told by the Salvationist:—

"By day we lay concealed in the corn or grass fields, and by night we crept along without any guide, hoping, and praying—I've prayed many times in the past, but never so much as on these nights—that all would come out right. On the first day we were fairly well; on the second we were very hungry; on the third our tongues were hanging out, and two of my comrades went mad.... On the fourth night we fell in with a British ambulance section, and were taken into camp. As I was passing the ambulance tent I heard someone singing:—

'I'm the child of a King,

I'm the child of a King;
With Jesus, my Saviour,
I'm the child of a King.'

I asked who it was, and was told it was a Salvationist. In the stillness of another night from one of the tents I heard:—

'Then we'll roll the old chariot along,
And we won't drag on behind.'

I tell you it was thrilling; it made me dance for joy. Two or three Salvationists were having a free-and-easy; after the chorus had been sung twice or so, I heard it taken up by other Salvationists in other tents, and presently from many parts of the camp could be heard the old Salvation song. It was splendid!"

III

CO. Bowen, Farrier Staff-Sergeant:—"I am a bandsman of Regina Corps and enlisted 13 months ago with the express purpose of trying to bring before the men of the C.E.F. the claims of Jesus Christ, and to impress upon them the joy of his glorious salvation. During those past months I am indeed glad to be able to testify to God's grace and strength at all times.

I arrived in France last January [1915] and was sent to the Ypres salient. I found very few men who were standing up for Christ, so I at once commenced to hold some Salvation Army meetings. Varied have been the places in which I have held services: barns, stables, farmhouses and huts. It is with a certain amount of satisfaction I can report that God has been pleased to use my feeble efforts. Many of the men, I am glad to say, have testified of their desire to serve Christ. Out here, where one is always within the sound of the guns, and is the object of attack by hostile aircraft, the need of being ready for the call to meet God at any moment is very forcibly brought home to the men.

Our meetings have been held sometimes under shell-fire, and it would do your hearts good, back home in dear old Canada, if you could hear the boys sing the grand old songs of praise to God with the assistance of a mandolin. We have had glorious times; many of the men have asked me during the week if I would offer prayer on their behalf. I have distributed the *War Cry*s and hundreds of copies of Christian literature of all descriptions which I have had sent over from England.

The Sunday previous a sergeant came into my tent after the service, and, for the first time for years, knelt down and prayed for himself. I am the only Salvationist in 600 men, yet I do feel so glad that God has given me courage to witness for him, and I pray that any other Salvationist, who may read these few lines, will launch out for Christ amongst their comrades."

We could go on reciting such vivid and inspiring stories of Salvationist soldiers in the trenches who "let their light so shine" that many others were brought to a realization of their spiritual needs. But they are, perhaps, all summed up in the story of one remarkable young Salvationist, Peter Houghton, from Galt, Ont. He was 24 years old when he enlisted on September 22, 1914, and later won a Distinguished Conduct Medal. His story was carried by the Detroit *News* after one of its reporters had interviewed a soldier recovering from wounds in a London, Ont., hospital and had asked who was one of the bravest men he knew. The soldier replied that, for him, Peter Houghton was and went on to say that:

Peter was a member of the village Salvation Army. We expected he'd be a kind of joy-killer in the trenches. Beneath his uniform he wore a red flannel shirt with the letters "S.A." on it. He carried a small copy of the Bible in his tunic.

But Pete didn't turn out to be a joy-killer. We soldiers are a rough lot, but he mixed with us like a brother. When we swore he had nothing to say about it. Only he didn't swear. When we gambled, Peter preached us no long sermons. Only he didn't gamble. When we stole each other's clothes, he had no remarks to make about morals. Only he left the other guy's duds alone. Peter preached only by example.

Peter had prayed every night on board ship, and over at Salisbury Plain. We thought he'd quit it when he got to the trenches. I'll never forget our first night. It was wet there—the water was well over our ankles.

In this water was a mess of discarded equipment, decayed food and dead rats that the boys killed with their rifle stocks. Maybe there were other forgotten dead things down there—I don't know. Anyway, it was an awful mess.

But Peter flopped down on his knees, in it just the same, folded his dirty, powder-stained hands together and asked God to save us from fire and sword, from the pestilence that flieth by noon-day, etc.

I remember that Peter had just got to the part about fire and sword, when a shell cut a blazing path of scarlet through the blue-black of the trench and lit up Peter, his folded hands and bared head just as though he were kneeling by the big drum back on the street corner in Galt, with the village lights twinkling on his Salvation Army clothes. Peter never stirred for the shell, but stayed right there soaking up the water in that foul, stinking trench. He never stirred when the boys twittered and groaned mockingly the way they do at some of the revival meetings.

Every night Peter prayed. Ridicule couldn't stop him. You might just as well have laughed at the cathedral in Ypres as laugh at Peter. He cared no more for jeer than he did for an enemy bayonet. Peter was brave. We knew all the time that Peter was brave, but we didn't think he was quite as brave as he turned out to be.

Peter was brave, even though he never had a bad word to say about the Germans. He never fought the enemy with his tongue. But he was right there with the bayonet in a charge with the best of us. He was right there, too, whenever volunteers were called for to go back through a hail of shells for grub. Going on a ration party is no picnic, believe me.

Many a man gets his death going to get something to keep him and the rest of the battalion alive.

Peter never let a married man, or a man who had a mother back home depending on him, go on a ration party if he was free to take his place. Peter would serve on the equally dangerous listening patrols, or the gruesome burial parties, any odd time he was asked to—and lots of times when he wasn't.

Peter's face always shone. It had a kind of beam that seemed to cheer you up. You felt when you looked at Peter's face that somewhere men weren't killing each other. He'd just clap his eyes on you, and if you'd been out all night in a soaking rain, without food for hours, and had just been ordered to do it all over again, you'd take a deep long breath, and go to it like a man. Peter's face gave you a new heart. The boys liked Peter, for all his prayers and hymns.

But it was at the second battle of Ypres that Peter showed the stuff that was in him. [You know] all about that fight, the long charge over the fields, the ditch, the cattle grazing near them, and the charges where we locked bayonets with the enemy and stabbed till one or the other of these groups of fighting, cursing, sweaty men gave way. Peter was there up front all the time. He fought, but he never cursed.

In one of these charges Captain Tom Lockhart had been hit.

We had no time to stop, even for a captain. We wouldn't have stopped if he'd been a general. We couldn't stop. It was a charge, and you don't stop in a charge. We just parted and swerved around him, leaving him lying there all huddled up in a heap and gasping out a stream of crimson on the green grass around him.

Well, in that particular charge we found we were up against machine guns. A machine gun ripping out 650 shots a minute just mows men down as a scythe mows down hay. It cut into us like a rip-saw and we had to fall back or be annihilated....

Well, Peter fought no more that day. By this time the

shattered battalion had been thrown back into some kind of shape, and Houghton found an officer with authority to relieve him from any more charging. Instead he volunteered to the far more dangerous task of going with a stretcher over that shell-swept field and gathering up the wounded, whose groans we heard all around us.

People back home think of stretcher-bearers as in some way exempt from the fire. But they aren't. They are more exposed to it. They go out in the open spaces where the worst of the hell is and pick up the wounded men. They are just fighting men from the battalion. They wear no insignia, no cross, no red band, nothing to distinguish them—even if the gunners back of the lines could see such signs. And the gunners can't see. They just hail shells on everything living that shows itself within the enemy lines, especially on stretcher parties.

I went forward into more charges that day, and I can't tell in detail about Peter's coming and goings across that field of fire. But I know he got dozens of wounded men out of that hell, and into the dressing station.

He did so much and risked so much that day that we cheered him when he came back to our trench. He was mud-stained, drenched to the skin from hauling men across that dirty ditch which divided the field, bloody from head to foot where the wounds of those he saved had gushed over him like fountains, but his face shone with the beam that seemed to light up the whole man.

Peter wasn't proud. He was just happy that he'd been able to do it. We cheered till we were hoarse, and Peter just smiled kind of modest like, and went to work making the wounded and dying men in our trench easier.

Peter got the Distinguished Conduct Medal for what he did, so the whole thing's a matter of record and you can look it up for yourself if you like. The best part, though, is what happened when we made Peter take his turn for a snatch of sleep in the dugout.

Peter dropped down to his knees in the soggy stream of

crimson in the bottom of that foul ditch, and when he had finished about the fire and sword, the pestilence that walketh at noon-day, and all the rest of his usual evening prayer, something unusual happened. No one snickered [*War Cry*, March 4, 1916].

Just how many Canadian Salvationists served in the First World War is not exactly known, though it is estimated that more than 2,000 did. When Britain declared war on Germany on August 4, 1914, they, like so many other young Canadian men, rushed to enlist, feeling that it was their duty to support the Mother Country in its fight against a perceived evil. By the war's end, on November 11, 1918, they were part of a contingent of more than 430,000 men and women who served overseas, of whom approximately 61,000 were killed and another 130,000 were wounded (many crippled for life).

Many Salvation Army corps across the nation were nearly depleted of their male congregation—and especially so were their brass bands. Thirty men from St. Thomas, Ont., 21 from Hamilton I, Ont., more than 30 from London Citadel, Ont., 15 from Edmonton Citadel and the list could go on. "In 1918," writes one historian, "almost every community mourned a generation lost to the killing fields of Flanders and the Somme, marking their sacrifices with monuments, statues, and cenotaphs across the dominion" [Tim Cook, *The Sharp End* (2007): 5]. And, in many Salvation Army halls, the honour rolls still remind us of the many who never did return to the fellowship of their corps or band.

But, beyond the call of duty noted by those honour rolls, is a record of Christian commitment that is not evident from the brief citations. For the most part, Canadian Salvationists did not abandon their evangelistic commitment in the face of so much evil and unbelief. Many of them became bandsmen in their battalions' brass bands—and more than a dozen Canadian Salvation Army bandmasters became battalion bandmasters—but they gave evidence of their religious convictions, as we have seen, by becoming unofficial chaplains in their smaller units, holding sing-songs, meetings and giving comfort wherever possible. It was yet another example of the manner in which the Army's evangelistic spirit was kept alive in the face of much pressure not to do so.

www.ingramcontent.com/pod-product-compliance
Lightning Source LLC
LaVergne TN
LVHW021453080426
835509LV00018B/2270